PENNINE DRAGON

THE REAL KING ARTHUR OF THE NORTH

SIMON KEEGAN

PENNINE DRAGON

First Edition
Published 2016
NEW HAVEN PUBLISHING LTD
www.newhavenpublishingltd.com
newhavenpublishing@gmail.com

Cover design © Pete Cunliffe
pcunliffe@blueyonder.co.uk

Copyright © 2016 Simon Keegan
All rights reserved
ISBN:
ISBN: 978-1-910705-32-2

Dedicated to my mum and dad

Contents

BOOK 2: BEARMAN PENDRAGON

Introduction

King Arthur is the greatest mythological folk hero who ever lived. For 1500 years the name of King Arthur has been familiar as Britain's greatest ever king and warrior. He is more famous than Robin Hood, William Tell, Charlemagne and Ivanhoe, but an accurate account of his real life has not been told until now.

Unlike many other heroes, Arthur comes with a cast of characters - the dashing Lancelot, the wizard Merlin, his magic sword Excalibur and the heroic Knights of the Round Table.

And our quest for the truth has never waned. Who were these people really?

Despite being a popular folk hero and subject of many movies, most people can't seem to agree on who this King Arthur was. He is often considered a myth, a fabrication, an amalgamation or equated with other later rulers.

But he was very much a real person - one who is indeed recorded in history - if you know where to look.

Any real King Arthur would have lived in around 500AD – the Dark Ages, but is seemingly not directly mentioned in the history books of the time.

A generation or two after he would have lived he is mentioned in numerous sources - and all of a sudden, kings all over the country began to name their sons 'Arthur' as if in tribute to a famous man of the same name.

He becomes a shining example of a British warlord, a hero in almost every Welsh folk tale and the names of his warriors are paid tribute to across the land.

Arthur suddenly came into vogue, and this is for good reason - his exploits were those of a real man.

But the question is not just whether Arthur existed. It's who he was. Was he a chivalrous king, a brutal warlord or a valiant emperor?

In early records, Arthur was the saviour of Britain after the Romans left, he defeated the Saxon invaders in 12 battles, culminating in the Battle of Badon - which is recorded in contemporary history.

In later Welsh folklore he is given companions like Culhwch, Gwalchmai, Cai and Bedwy. These characters may not be well known to modern fans, but maybe Lancelot, Merlin, Galahad, Tristan and Excalibur are.

For 1,500 years we have not tired of tales of Arthur. There have been Hollywood blockbusters like Excalibur, King Arthur, Tristan and Isolde, First Knight and now the Camelot TV series.

But who was the real Arthur? Who were his parents? What battles did he really fight? Did he really live at Camelot? Did he really have friends like Lancelot, Gawain and Merlin, and enemies like Mordred?

This dynamic new book will rewrite the history of King Arthur. The book shows that Arthur was neither a Cornish prince, nor a mythological god - he was in fact the king of Northern Britain, ruling the Pennines, York and up to Hadrian's Wall.

This book not only identifies Arthur, Lancelot and Guinevere but also knights like Galahad, Gawain, Mordred and Perceval. As well as meeting Merlin, Morgan and Uther Pendragon, we also discover the real Camelot, the Lady of the Lake, Excalibur and the Round Table.

For the first time, every single aspect of Arthurian lore is proven in one historic analysis, tied together in one man's life. Unlike Richard the Lionheart, William Wallace and Alfred the Great, in Arthur's case the sheer volume of mythology surrounding him makes many assume he was not an historic warleader - despite evidence to the contrary.

Contemporary historian St Gildas refers to the Battle of Badon as the greatest defeat of the Saxons by the Britons, and two later history books independently name Arthur as the commander at Badon. He is also named in a con-temporary war poem - The Gododdin, where a great Celtic king is described as valiant in his victories against the Saxons "although he was no Arthur."

That Arthur's rank was listed as "Dux Bellorum" does not prevent him from having been a King, any more than the Duke of

Wellington's having been prime minister prevented him from being commander at Waterloo and of course a Duke.

This book primarily shows that Arthur was a real, genuine celtic warleader and king. It also reveals that Arthur was listed in the Celtic Genealogies all along. Many historians "missed" him because they assumed he was Cornish or Welsh.

This is the tale of the real King Arthur. And it is published on the 1500th anniversary of the Battle of Badon, Arthur's greatest victory over the Saxons in 516AD.

What are the unprejudiced facts about Arthur?

1) There is no contemporary reference to King Arthur, except for possibly by the nickname The Bear (In Welsh bear is *Arth*) by Gildas. This may locate him in central Wales.

2) A stone dated to Arthur's time and found at Tintagel castle in Cornwall refers to an Artognou. This may locate him to Cornwall.

3) Two hundred years before Arthur, there was a Roman commander garrisoned at Hadrian's Wall called Lucius Artorius Castus. This may locate him in the north.

4) Gildas makes reference to a battle called Badon but doesn't name the leader. He seems to suggest it was in around 500AD, give or take 20 years. It has been suggested this was Bath.

5) Bards considered to have lived around the same time as Arthur, or slightly later, including Aneirin, Llywarch Hen and Taliesin, are credited as having mentioned him but did not give explicit dates or places, nor are original manuscripts surviving. These bards are associated with the north.

6) The Annales Cambrae and Nennius, from a few hundred years later, attribute the Battle of Badon to Arthur, along with other battles which may be located at various points across the country.

7) The Annales Cambrae dates Badon to 516 and Camlan to 539. Although it has been suggested these dates are around 15 years too late, a lifespan of around 470-540 seems likely.

8) Some of Arthur's battles would seem to be against the Saxons (or Angles, Jutes etc) while at least some may be against British or Scots enemies.

9) Within the next three generations after Arthur would have lived, kings around the country called their sons "Arthur", including Arthur of Dyfed, Artuir of Dalriads, Athrwys of Gwent and Arthmael of Brittany. This suggests Arthur's fame may have been national.

10) The earliest references to Arthur give him various titles including Nennius who calls him "Dux Bellorum" (battle duke) and says he fought with the kings of Britain.

The Legend of Arthur

The Dark Ages... After the last of the Romans left, Britain was divided and without a king, a time when usurping tyrants like King Vortigern emerged, as well as generals like Ambrosius. The foolish tyrant Vortigern invited the Saxons to Britain as mercenaries, and they betrayed the Britons in the original Night of the Long Knives. But Vortigern's wizard Merlin foretold that the Red Dragon of Britain would rise again, and subsequently Uther Pendragon, the brother of Ambrosius, became king. But, although he was a mighty ruler, Uther was not the king to unify Britain. He slept with Igraine, the wife of his rival Duke, Gorlois, and, as a result, baby Arthur was born - in around 470AD - the illegitimate heir to the king.

Merlin took Arthur from his parents and had the wise Sir Ector raise him as his own with foster brother Kay and friend Bedevere.

Igraine and Gorlois' daughter Morgan would later prove to be a thorn in the side of her half brother. When he was around 15, Arthur received his famous sword Excalibur and was proclaimed King of the Britons, ruling from Camelot. He and his companions like Llwch (later Lancelot), Culhwch, Kay and Bedevere had many adventures across Britain and Ireland, and Arthur met his bride Gwenhwyfar (Guinevere). Together they are credited with various sons including Cynvelyn, Amhar, Llacheu and Gwydre.

Arthur faced challenges from invaders on all sides - Saxons, Irish, Picts, Scots and Franks and his own rebellious kinsmen, but he was able to defeat his enemies in 12 battles culminating in the siege of Badon.

Around his famous Round Table were warriors like Lancelot, his father Ban and his son Galahad; Gawain; Kay; Bedevere; Perceval; Cador; Ector; Tristan and rival rulers like King Mark, King Melkin and King Uriens.

Within the kingdom there were many romances, the adultery between Lancelot and Guinevere and Tristan and Isolde as well as Culhwch and Olwen.

Eventually Arthur met his rebellious relative Mordred, (either his brother, son or nephew) who he fought at Camlann. After the battle, Arthur gave his sword to one of his knights, (Bedevere or Perceval) who then threw it into the lake.

Arthur left his kingdom to the son of his kinsman Cador, but eventually the Saxons were victorious and the Celtic Britons foretold that their King Arthur would come again, he was the Once and Future King.

The Search for Arthur

This study is about separating the fact from the fiction and looking at Arthur in his most historical form. Like Wellington and Waterloo, or Nelson and Trafalgar, the one battle with which Arthur is associated is Badon.

The Wikipedia page on Badon says:

Battle of Badon
Date: Unknown circa 500AD
Location: Unknown, various locations possible
Result: Strategic British victory; Saxon expansion halted by many decades
Belligerents: Briton - Anglo Saxons
Commanders and leaders: Unknown, possibly Arthur

This information, or rather lack of it, hits the nail on the head. We know Badon was a rare battle, in that the Britons (ie the Celts) were able to soundly defeat the Saxons to such a point that their invasion was stunted. And we know of no other candidate for who commanded the Britons than Arthur.

Badon is mentioned in historic sources such as De Excidio Britannae (The Ruin of Britain) by Gildas and the Ecclesiastic History of the English People by Bede. Neither of these sources name Arthur as the commander, but by the same token, they don't offer anybody else, and somebody must have commanded the Britons.

The later Annales Cambrae dates it as 516AD, and tells us the commander was Arthur, as does the Historia Brittonum (attributed to Nennius). Nennius tells us Arthur was Dux Bellorum (Duke of Battles) and commanded the Kings of Britain. If Nennius substituted Arthur's name in place of someone else who also won the battle, then he also must have destroyed every single record of the battle - because nobody is ever associated with winning it but Arthur. In other words there are multiple

14

sources that link Arthur with Badon and nothing that links anybody else with it. Prior to Nennius and the Annales Cambrae, we had only heard the name Arthur in brief mentions, such as bards alluding to his battle valour. The early Arthur was therefore a battle leader, a man who commanded the kings of Britain against the invading Saxons in 516AD. This is the man we are trying to find.

Sources frequently referred to in this book include:

"Gildas" - De Excidio Britannia - written circa 550AD
"Nennius" - Historia Brittonum - written circa 830AD
"Annales Cambrae" - written circa 980AD

Other bardic sources include the works of Taliesin, Aneirin and Llywarch Hen, who may have lived in around Arthur's time, but surviving manuscripts are much newer.

The Riddle of Arthur

"This is that Arthur of whom the trifling of the Britons talks such nonsense, even today; a man clearly worthy not to be dreamed of in fallacious fables, but to be proclaimed in veracious histories, as one who long sustained his tottering country and gave the shattered minds of his fellow citizens an edge for war."
William of Malmesbury (1095-1143)

Many of King Arthur's exploits are fantasy, myth and folklore. But the same is true of Charlemagne, Alfred the Great, Miyamoto Musashi and Bruce Lee, but nobody ever suggests they did not exist. The reason why many doubt the existence of Arthur is not because of his fantastic exploits but because there has never been a coin found that reads "Artorius Rex" nor has there ever been a convincing grave found that reads "King Arthur lies here" in 6th century script. Nor is he mentioned in contemporary records.

However it is very difficult to prove a negative in this way. For one, there are only really two existing books from Arthur's time and neither are comprehensive. One is the Anglo Saxon Chronicle, written by his enemies, and the other is a religious rant by a monk named Gildas.

The evidence that Arthur never existed is flimsy compared to the evidence that he did. For one, Gildas hardly names anyone, and when he does he uses word play and imagery. He likens three kings to dragons and dogs but he also mentions one called The Bear. When we consider that Bear in Welsh is Arth, it seems very likely that Gildas did in fact allude to Arthur. For example, a few generations after Arthur's time two independent sources, one known as 'Nennius' and the other known as the 'Annales Cambrae' refer to Arthur as having been the victor of a Battle of Badon which was mentioned by Gildas.

So we know from Gildas that Badon was fought, yet he doesn't name the British commander. It seems perverse to doubt that the only man named as victor of that battle was not the victor.

16

Then, a few generations after Arthur would have lived, there was an otherwise inexplicable trend. Kings of Britain began calling their eldest sons Arthur. There was Artur son of Aedan in Argyll, there was Arthur son of Pedr and Arthur son of Bicuir in Dyfed, there was Athrwys son of Meurig in Gwent and there was even Arthmael in Brittany.

The likelihood of course is that the Battle of Badon, dated to around 516AD was won by a man named Arthur. This man would have been born in around 470 or 480, began his active service in around 500, flourished in around 520 and probably commanded his last battle in around 540, aged 60 or 70.

From Nennius we also get a mention of Arthur's son Anir. The Annales Cambrae doesn't name any relatives but place Arthur in a battle with somebody called Medraut or Mordred who has a British rather than Saxon name but is assumed to be an enemy. Of course in latest Arthurian legends both Amhar and Mordred do indeed feature.

In Nennius, the Annales, and what can be inferred by Gildas, Arthur is placed chronologically shortly after British leader Ambrosius Aurelianus and before Saxon leader Ida. So we can suggest a lifetime of about 470-540 for Arthur, therefore men like Artur of Dalriada, Athrwys of Gwent and Arthur of Dyfed lived too late. Riothamus and Ambrosius lived too early. The only other candidates from the right generation are Owain Ddantgwyn and Cadell, but neither of those are as convincing as a king called Arthur.

Furthermore the Annales Cambrae gives two battles - Badon in 516 or 518 and Camlann in about 539 or 541. Frustratingly, Arthur and Ambrosius (whose existence is not in doubt since he is mentioned by Gildas), do not feature in the geneological king lists. Therefore, suggesting Arthur as a son or nephew of Ambrosius is not helpful. So we look to the oldest Welsh mythologies and find quite a few relatives for Arthur.

In the earliest stories with relatives listed for Arthur, he is credited with various kinsmen and often he is a background character to their adventures. His mother is Eigyr (Igraine or Ygerne) and he has a kinsman called Culhwch (or Einion) and a sister called Anna or Gwyar. Through Eigyr and her siblings Arthur has various cousins but Culhwch is the one about whom most is written.

The style of the Culhwch story is much like an old Irish folklore, as he goes on a quest for somewhat magical items, while Arthur is in the background as a king. Anna is usually described as married to a Scottish king (the prototype Lot of Lothian) and is the mother of Gwalchmai or Gawain. Arthur's maternal grandfather is a chieftain called Amlawdd Gwledig.

It is almost as if the Arthur who features in Welsh folklore like Culhwch and Olwen is at a very different time in his life to the man who fought at Badon. At Badon, Arthur was following in the footsteps of Ambrosius, the last of the Romans and clashing with the Saxons - whereas the Arthur in Welsh folklore is a much more settled king. He is involved in petty squabbles and quests, settling disputes over pigs, cows and tables.

It is typical of Welsh storytelling that Arthur's mother Eigyr, his cousin Culhwch and maternal grandfather Amlawdd are viewed as significant, whereas his father and paternal grandfathers are not. However, in later stories the more patriarchal storytelling begins to reveal male characters in his family tree. Geoffrey of Monmouth, who claimed to have access to a very old Welsh book, tells us that Arthur's father was Uther Pendragon, second husband of Igraine (after Gorlois) and that Uther was the brother of Ambrosius Aurelianus. Unfortunately, Uther is neither recorded in genealogies nor identified as Arthur's father in Welsh sources – he is however named in a few celtic legends - so Geoffrey did not invent Uther. And there is nothing in these old tales to say Uther was not Arthur's father - or Eigyr's husband - so maybe Geoffrey did have access to other British tales.

Geoffrey tells us that Uther and Ambrosius were the sons of the Emperor Constantine (Flavius Claudius Constantinus known in Britain as Constantine III) – but this poses a problem of its own. Constantine died in 411AD, therefore Uther would have been born in around 400AD, too early to be the father of Arthur born in around 470 or 480. Flavius Claudius Constantinus was a

Roman general who declared himself Western Roman Emperor in Britannia in 407 and established himself in Gaul. Recognised by the Emperor Honorius in 409, collapsing support and military setbacks saw him abdicate in 411. He was captured and executed shortly afterwards.

This gap is usually filled by giving Ambrosius and Uther an older brother called Constans and inserting another king named Vortigern, but this doesn't seem to help much either. The later genealogies ('genealogies of the heroes') which do list Arthur and Uther confuse the matter further, because they muddle up Emperor Constantine III with the Cornish king Constantine who was one generation younger than Arthur so could hardly have been the man's grandfather!

The excellent article From Glein to Camlann, on the website Vortigern Studies, sums it up:

"There are those who would follow the genealogy offered for Uther found in Geoffrey of Monmouth. In that source, Uther was the son of Constantine III, the western emperor who was proclaimed in 407 by British troops. Uther's brothers are said to be Constans and Aurelius Ambrosius. As it so happens, Constantine III did have a son Constans, but Aurelius Ambrosius is an anachronism, for that personage was the 4th century prefect of Gaul, father of the much more famous St. Ambrose.

"The reason for the anachronism is simple: the 5th century Constantine III took his name – Flavius Claudius Constantinus – from the 4th century Constantine I the Great. The latter Constantine also had a son named Constans (337-350). This Constans had brothers named Constantius II (337-361) and Constantine II (337-340).

"The 5th century Constantine III had a younger son named Julian. But both Julian and Constans were killed on the Continent, the first at Arles in 411 and the latter at Vienne. Although there is some reason to believe that Constans and Julian may originally have borne British names, for chronological reasons alone neither of these two sons of Constantine III could have been Uther Pendragon.

"So if Constantine III was not the father of Uther, and neither Constans nor Ambrosius were the brothers of Uther, how do we possibly find out what kingdom Uther ruled in Britain?

"The Welsh genealogy for Arthur follows Geoffrey in the main, making Arthur son of Uther son of Constantine the Blessed (W. Fendigaid) or 'of Cornwall' (W. Cernyw, Corneu) son of Cynfor son of Tudwal son of Gwrfawr son of Gadeon son of Eudaf. The sole purpose of this Welsh genealogy, it would appear, was to provide Constantine, father of Uther, with a Breton origin. This may have been done (although see below) in order to accommodate Geoffrey's claim that Constantine came from Brittany.

"This genealogy is patently false. Cynfor, the supposed grandfather of Uther, is the Cynfor/Cunomorus, Prince of Domnonee in Brittany and probably of Dumnonia in southwestern Britain, who died c.560."

Cynfor/Cunomorus was first identified with "King Mark" or March by the Breton monk Wrmonoc in his Life of St. Paul of Leon, written in 884. We are told Arthur and March son of Meirchion are first cousins in The Dream of Rhonabwy. But it was actually another March, son of Meirchion, that Arthur was related to, as we will see later.

David Nash Ford from Early British Kingdoms sums up:

"Welsh tradition also sees Arthur as High-King of Britain but tends to follow the genealogies laid down in the Mostyn MS117 and the Bonedd yr Arwr. These show Arthur as grandson of Constantine but, this time, he is Constantine Corneu, the King of Dumnonia. Traditional Arthurian legend records three Kings of Dumnonia during Arthur's reign: Constantine's son, Erbin; grandson, Gereint and great grandson, Cado. Nowhere is there any indication that these three were closely related to Arthur, nor that he had any claim on the Dumnonian Kingdom. Nor is there any explanation as to why a Dumnonian prince would have been raised to the High-Kingship of Britain. Arthur's connection with this area of Britain is purely due to his supposedly being conceived at Tintagel, the residence of his mother's first husband,

and buried at Glastonbury, the most ancient Christian site in the country."

So, we have a number of questions:

1) Who was Uther Pendragon? And was he the father of King Arthur?

2) Was Ambrosius Aurelianus the brother of Uther Pendragon?

3) What "Constantine" was the father of Uther and Ambrosius?

4) Who was Eigyr and who was her father Amlawdd?

5) Who were Gawain and Culhwch?

We must note at this point we are not concerned with the likes of Sir Lancelot, Morgan Le Fay and Merlin the Wizard. At this stage of our quest, we simply want to place Arthur in history and in a family pedigree. All of these questions will be answered, but in order to seek out these people we need to know where to look. And so we start at the beginning.

PENNINE DRAGON

BOOK ONE
PENNINE DRAGON

"King Arthur lives in merry Carlisle, And seemely is to see,
And there with him Queene Geney,
That bride soe bright of blee complexion."

PENNINE DRAGON

The Evidence

Sources:

- De Excidio Britanniae by Gildas, c.540
- The Gododdin by Anieirin, C590
- The Battle of Llongborth by Llywarch Hen, c.600
- Historia Brittonum by Nennius, c.830
- Annales Cambriae, c. 970
- The Stanzas of the Graves, c1000
- Legend of St. Goeznovius, c. 1019
- The Life of St Cadoc, 1075
- The Life of St Carannog, 1100
- The Life of St Illtud
- Culhwch and Olwen, 1100
- Pa Gur, 1100
- Taliesin, 1100
- The Triads, 1100
- The Modena carvings, 1120
- William of Malmesbury, 1125
- Arthur and the Eagle, 1130
- Geoffrey of Monmouth, 1138
- The Life of St Padarn, 1150
- The Life of St Gildas, 1150
- The Exhumation of Arthur's Body, c.1193
- The Triads, c1100s
- The Dream of Rhonabwy, c.1200

FROM GILDAS: In the late 5th century a "proud tyrant" (usually identified with Vortigern) invited the Saxons to Britain as mercenaries but was then betrayed by them.

The country was defended against the Saxons by Ambrosius.

The greatest defeat of the Saxons was at a battle called Badon.

A generation after Badon, five rulers were Maelgwyn (the dragon), Vortipor (the protector), Aurelius Caninus, Constantine and Cuneglasus. The latter was once charioteer to someone called the Bear - in Welsh, Arth. This establishes Arthur in the generation between Ambrosius and Maelgwyn (so 470-540)

FROM ANEIRIN: A generation or two after Arthur, a Northern British leader is considered a great leader for his valiant battles against the Saxons, but his deeds don't compare to those of Arthur. This supports Arthur as a war leader, someone known in the north and of a previous generation.

FROM NENNIUS: After Ambrosius and Vortigern (Gildas' proud tyrant) Arthur was Dux Bellorum (Leader of Battles) and led the British kings in 12 winning battles against the Saxons, the last of which was Badon. After Arthur, Ida took Bernicia (in 547). Another work in the anthology describes Arthur killing his son Anir in Archenfield.

FROM ANNALES CAMBRAE: Arthur defeated the Saxons at the battle of Badon in 516 or 518. In 539 or 541 he and Medraut (presumably his enemy) were killed at the battle of Camlan.

From these sources and other reliable histories we can gain the following timeline:

Generation 1
The Magnus Maximus Generation (the time of Arthur's great great great grandfather) Born circa 350, ruled circa 380, died circa 400

Generation 2
The Constantine III Generation (the time of Arthur's great great grandfather) Born circa 370, ruled circa 400, died circa 430

Generation 3
The Coel Hen Generation (the time of Arthur's great grandfather) Born circa 390, ruled circa 430, died circa 460

Generation 4
The Cunedda and Vortigern Generation (the time of Arthur's grandfather) Born circa 420, ruled circa 450, died circa 480

Generation 5
The Ambrosius Aurelianius Generation (the time of Arthur's father) Born circa 450, ruled circa 470, died circa 520 - This is the generation of Arthur's father and uncles, and also includes British rulers like Einion Yrth

Generation 6
The King Arthur Generation Born circa 480, ruled circa 520, died circa 540 - This generation also includes British rulers like Cadwallon

Generation 7
The Maelgwyn Generation (the time of Arthur's sons) Born circa 510, ruled circa 550, died circa 570 - This generation also includes British rulers like Constantine, and Saxon rulers like Ida. It would also include Arthur's sons.

We should point out here that later historic Arthurs lived too far down the line to be the Arthur of Badon. The Scottish Artur Mac Gabran would belong to generation 8, the Dyfed Arthur ap Pedr to generation 9 and the Gwent Athrwys ap Meurig to generation 10.

Our King Arthur must have been born in generation 6, in other words born around 460-490. He must have been in a position to lead the Britons at Badon (500-520) and he must have been in a position to fight at Camlann (520-541). But everybody knows this is the time frame where Arthur must be placed, so why is it proving so hard to locate him? The reason is because most people begin their search in Dumnonia (Devon and Cornwall) or South Wales. These places have been exhausted as the home of the historical Arthur and he is nowhere to be found.

In order to track down the location of Arthur, we must go back a few generations and find out where he would have really lived.

Multiple Arthurs?

It may be possible that earlier Celtic rulers contributed to the overall Arthurian mythos. For example:

Arviragus supposedly married Genvissa of Rome (reminiscent of Arthur and a Roman Guanhumara)

Artorius Castus commanded a Sarmatian Cavalry (as seen in the Clive Owen movie)

Riothamus fought in Brittany and may have opposed Rome

Any number of similarly named men from Athrwys of Gwent to Artur of Dalriada may have accounted for small parts of the tales. For example - in one minor legend Arthur has a son called Morgan the black, and Athrwys had a son called Morgan. But only one man can have been the Arthur who commanded at Badon, who defeated the Saxons in 12 battles and fought Medraut at Camlann.

The original Arthur was a Dux Bellorum, a warlord.

It is this Arthur that we are discovering.

There was one King Arthur. Any other Arthurs are just the icing on the cake.

The original Merlin and Arthur

The first explicit mention of Arthur is in the poem The Gododdin by Aneirin. Here the poem tells of how the British Gododdin clans raised a force of about 300 men to assault the Angle stronghold of Catraeth, perhaps Catterick, North Yorkshire. One of the British leaders is compared to Arthur.

The first mention of Merlin (Myrddin) is in connection with the battle of Arthuret, again in the North Yorkshire area. The

Battle was fought, according to the Annales Cambriae, in 573. The main antagonists appear to have been Gwenddoleu ap Keidyaw and Peredur ap Eleuthr. Gwenddoleu was defeated and killed and his bard, Myrddin Wyllt, went mad and ran into the forest.

Gwenddolau was a Brythonic king in the area around Hadrian's Wall and Carlisle during the sub-Roman period in Britain. Carwinley, near Longtown, north of Carlisle is thought to represent Caer Wenddolau or Gwenddolau's Fort. So both the earliest Arthur, the earliest Merlin and - to a lesser extent the earliest Sir Percival, Peredur - were first cited as being based between North Yorkshire and Hadrian's Wall.

Even more incredibly we will show that Myrddin, Peredur, Gwenddolau and Aneirin were all related to one man - and that one man, the ruler of the area from Hadrian's Wall to Yorkshire, was the real King Arthur.

Since Arthur lived in the fifth and sixth centuries, our most valuable source should be the work of St Gildas, who compiled De Dexcidio Et Conquesto Britanniae (The Ruin and Conquest of Britain) in around 530-570. However, Gildas makes no mention of Arthur. He praises at length a leader called Ambrosius Aurelianus (a man who would have been contemporary with Gildas' grandfather) and then condemns five contemporary kings for their anti-christian behaviour.

"After this, sometimes our countrymen, sometimes the enemy, won the field, to the end that our Lord might in this land try after his accustomed manner these his Israelites, whether they loved him or not, until the year of the siege of Mount Badon when took place also the last almost, though not the least slaughter of our cruel foes." **Gildas (516AD-570AD)**

The kings berated by Gildas are:
- Maelgwyn of Gwynedd (North Wales
- Constantine of Damnonia (supposedly of Devon)
- Vortiporus of Demetia (Dyfed)

- Cuneglas of Rhos (perhaps of Powys)
- Aurelius Conanus (perhaps of Gloucester)

Genealogy stating Maelgwyn succeeded Arthur:

Llewelyn ap Gruffyd mab Llywelyn m. Ioruerth m. Owein m. Gruffyd m. Kynan m. Iago m. [Idwal m. Meuric m.] Idwal voel m. Anarawt m. Rodri m. Meruyn vrych, gwr priawt Esyllt verch Kynan Tindaethwy mab Rodri maelwynawc m. Idawl iwrch m. Katwaladyr vendigeit m. Katwallawn m. Katuan m. Iago m. Beli m. Run m. Maelgwn Gwyned, herwyd dull y beird. Namyn o herwyd yr Istoria Beli oed vab Eynyan vab **Maelgwn, y gwr a uu petweryd brenhin ar Ynys Prydein gwedy Arthur.**

Gildas himself was descended from a Pictish family in what is now Scotland, and moved to Wales to become a monk. Gildas liked to make puns on people's names and place names. He called Aurelius Conanus "caninus" suggesting he was a dog, referred to the Dumnonians and the "damnonians." He also calls Aurelius a lion's whelp, calls Boudicca a lioness, calls Vortipor a grey dog and Maelgwyn a dragon.

Gildas does it seem, allude to Arthur too in this way. He calls Cuneglas the "driver of the chariot of The Bear's stronghold, and since the Welsh for bear is Arth, this would not be lost on the reader of the time.

Could, then Cuneglas, prince of Rhos have once been subordinate to Arthur, and could this place Arthur near North Wales? Let's examine his genealogy. Cuneglas was the son of Owain, who, like Maelgwyn's father Cadwallon, was the son of Einion Yrth.

Einion Yrth was a man from the region which is now the North of England. His father was king Cunedda and his mother was Gwawl, daughter of Coel Hen.

Coel Hen and Cunedda were the most powerful kings of Northern Britain. Coel was the Dux Brittaniarum (warleader of Britain), based at York and defending the length of Hadrian's

Wall, and Cunedda was the king of the northern Gododdin territory (modern north-east England and south-east Scotland). Britain reported to a Magister Militum in Gaul, then the highest ranks were:

- Commes Britanniarum - Count of Britain

- Commes Litoris Saxonicii - Count of the Saxon Shore

- Dux Britanniarum - Duke of Britain

Aneirin's Gododdin

The Gododdin was made famous by the Northern British bard Aneirin. Again, the allusion to Arthur is brief but significant. He praises a warrior for his valour and adds "but he was no Arthur", implying he ranked Arthur's martial valour very highly. Here we have no reason to think Arthur was any kind of a mythological figure - Guaurthur named in the Gododdin was a war leader from the north, and so it is likely Arthur was the same.

He thrust beyond three hundred, most bold,
He cut down the centre and far wing.
He proved worthy, leading noble men;
He gave from his herd steeds for winter.
He brought black crows to a fort's all, though he was not Arthur.
He made his strength a refuge, the front line's bulwark, Gwawrddur.

Like Gildas and Cuneglas, we should look at Aneirin's pedigree:

Coel
Ceneu
Pabo
Dunaut
Aneirin

So we have Pictish prince Gildas, linking Arthur to Cuneglas of North Wales, whose family were descended from Coel; and

31

then we have Aneirin who was descended from Coel, mentioning Arthur. So if Gildas was a man of the north, and Cuneglas was descended from the men of the north, and Aneirin was a man of the north it is seemingly possible Arthur too was a man of the north.

The earliest mentions of both Arthur and Myrddin are in the North Yorkshire area. There is nothing here to suggest Arthur was from Cornwall or Devon - so far all signs are pointing to either what is now North Wales or what is now the north of England. But this is hardly evidence in itself. What of our first two major references to Arthur - Nennius and the Annales Cambrae.

Nennius and the Annales Cambrae

The first substantial historic reference to Arthur comes from the 8th or 9th century monk called Nennius, who called Arthur "Dux Bellorum" (battle leader) and says he led the kings of Britain into 12 battles against the Saxons. This would tie in with Gildas' comment that King Cuneglas drove a chariot for "the Bear".

The 12 battles are also fairly certainly Northern battles, including York, Scotland and Durham. These are identified in a later chapter. The point at this stage is that in early references, Arthur is a war leader, seemingly linked to the north of Britain. The 12th battle, Mount Badon was mentioned by Gildas following his paragraph on Ambrosius but again not identified. The Annales Cambrae attributes two battles to Arthur, Badon in 516 or 518 and Camlan in 539 or 541. Again, in a later chapter I identify Camlan with Camboglanna, a site along Hadrian's Wall.

Once again, we can see Arthur linked to the north of England. He is taken further north by Lambert of St Omer in circa 1100 who calls him the "King of the leader of the Picts". Here it is likely that he interpreted Nennius' comment that "Arthur fought with the Kings of Britain" to mean he could not be British himself. Arthur is seen as a military warleader not a deity.

Llywarch and Taliesin

The next references to Arthur we have are from Llywarch Hen and Taliesin, the court bards of Cumbrian ruler Urien Rheged.

These could actually pre-date Nennius and the Annales but the existing manuscripts do not.

In the "Elegy for Gereint", Llywarch calls Arthur "imperator", a title meaning emperor, and again suggesting he was senior to kings. In the poem "The Chair of the Sovereign" Taliesin refers to Arthur as "the Guletic around the old renowned boundary" which places Arthur as guletic (protector) along Hadrian's Wall.

Once again, Arthur is tied to the north of England, but significantly there is that sense he was not only a king but of an emperor-like status.

Like Coel Hen, Arthur, as the Imperator or Dux Bellorum, must have ruled from Hadrian's Wall across the land of the Goddodin.

Llywarch Hen was another descendant of Coel. His pedigree is:

Coel Hen
Ceneu
Gurgust
Eleuther
Llywarch Hen

So, from the early references to Arthur, it seems we are looking for not only a man born in our generation 6, but also a man who was:

1) A Dux Bellorum who led kings into battle
2) A ruler who succeeded Ambrosius Aurelianus
3) A ruler who defended Hadrian's wall and was based in the north
4) A successor of Coel Hen, as Dux Brittaniarum
5) The protagonist of the battle of Mount Badon in 516.
6) The protagonist of the battle of Camlan in circa 539.

Then we must discover how this person is related to:

1) Uther Pendragon and Igraine
2) Amlawdd Gwledig
3) Constantine
4) Ambrosius Aurelianus
5) Gawain, Culhwch and Modred

So we will start with Constantine and Coel...

Arthur's Predecessors

Birdoswald Roman fort: Hadrian's Wall

At one time, London shared its capital city distinction with another city. The city was York, capital of Brittania Inferior.

From the First Century AD to the start of the Fifth, Britain was part of the Roman Empire. By the time of the Roman conquest of Britain, the area was occupied by a tribe known to the Romans as the Brigantes. The Brigantian tribal area initially became a Roman client state, but, later its leaders became more hostile to Rome. As a result, the Roman Ninth Legion was sent north of the Humber into Brigantian territory.

The city itself was founded in 71 AD, when the Ninth Legion conquered the Brigantes and constructed a wooden military fortress on flat ground above the River Ouse, close to its confluence with the River Foss. The fortress, which was later rebuilt in stone, covered an area of 50 acres and was inhabited by 6,000 soldiers.

The Emperors Hadrian, Septimius Severus and Constantius I all held court in York during their various campaigns. During his stay, the Emperor Severus proclaimed York capital of the province of Britannia Inferior, and it is likely that it was he who granted York the privileges of a colonia or city.

Constantius I died in 306 AD during his stay in York, and his son Constantine the Great was proclaimed Emperor by the troops based in the fortress.

It seems strange now to think of York as a major part of the world's greatest empire, but three emperors were born or died there.

• Septimus Severus (Emperor of Rome 193AD-211AD) was born in Libya but died in York;

• Constantius (Emperor of Western Rome 305AD-306AD) was born in Illyricum and died in York;

• Constantine I (Emperor of Rome 306-337) was said to have been born in York.

Clearly, in the 4th century, York was not just significant in Britain, but in the Roman Empire. The Romans were conquerers but they led with the carrot rather than the stick. Many Britons came to think of themselves as Roman, many converted to Christianity. Rome gave civilisation and safety. The Romans had permitted British tribes to continue to worship their own gods and crown their own chieftains.

In 410, during the reign of Constantine III (Emperor of Britain and Gaul 407-411), the overall emperor of Rome, Honorius, withdrew his men from Britain as Rome was being sacked by the Visigoths. Therefore again, if Arthur was a successor of men like Constantine it would make sense for him to have York as a base. Gildas, Aneirin, Taliesin, Llywarch Hen, Nennius and the Annales Cambrae all support the idea Arthur was from the North, and the lives of Constantine and his family suggest the importance of York. Along with Hadrian's Wall this would seem to be the early Arthurian heartland.

It would show that an Arthur of York was indeed a successor of Constantine, by military might if not blood.

Coel Hen

In around 410AD with the exodus of the Romans, the British chieftain who was the strongest emerged as Coel Hen. He was the "old king Coel" of the nursery rhymes ("Old King Cole was a merry old soul"). Coel is sometimes called Coel Guotepauc (Coel Vortipor) - Coel the Protector. He was something between an emperor and a king - the strongest ruler in Britain and the founder of a dynasty - and again his stronghold was the north. Coel would have been born in around 380 in the north of Britain, almost certainly around Ebrauc (York) or Northumbria, near to Hadrian's Wall. He was a Romanised leader and the names of his family seem to suggest a link with Hadrian's Wall.

His father is thought to have been called Tegfan, his wife Ystradwal and his daughter Gwawl. The names of his wife and daughter are almost certainly plays on the word 'wall', as in Hadrian's Wall, which Coel would have defended against the Picts. It has been suggested that Coel was ranked as Dux Bellorum (Duke of Battles) or Dux Brittania (Duke of Britain). Some genealogies even make Coel the father-in-law of Constantine.

Britannia.com states: "Considering the regions over which Coel's supposed descendants ruled, his own sphere of influence must have covered a vast area, from Hadrian's Wall to the Southern Pennines. In fact, the exact area that would have been governed at this time by the Dux Britanniarum, a Roman official in charge of the military defence of Northern Britain. With his headquarters at York, he would have been in an ideal position to extend some semblance of Roman-type authority into the 5th century, long after the army and administration had returned to Italy."

Norma Goodrich writes: "As duke of Britain, so elected in plenary session by the British chieftains, Arthur would have commanded both the Antonine and the Hadrianic walls comprising 36 fortresses of the line and, after the year 446, the remnants of the 6th Roman Legion. His headquarters would have been their old station or the city and vast fort of Carlisle."

Coel's son Germanus ruled the southern Votadini territory. His son-in-law Cunedda ruled the northern Votadini, also called Gododdin, which is now Lothian. His son Ceneu controlled Ebrauc (York).

Cunedda's forefathers include names like Octern, Aeturnus and Paternus, suggesting he was a Roman who was later grafted into a Celtic pedigree. According to legends, Coel's base was Ayr, which was later named Kyle in his honour. For this reason his name may have been Ayr-Coel, Ayr Coll Lawhir or Agricola.

In one campaign against the Picts and the Irish Scots, the enemy fled to the hills ahead of Coel's army, who eventually set up camp at Kyle. For a long time, the British were triumphant but the enemy advanced an attack on Coel's stronghold. Coel and his men were taken by surprise, overrun and scattered.

It is said that Coel wandered the unknown countryside until he eventually got caught in a bog at Coilsfield (in Tarbolton, Ayrshire) and drowned.

Coel was first buried in a mound there before being removed to the church at Coylton. After his death, Coel's Northern Kingdom was divided between two of his sons, Ceneu and Germanus. Again, like Cunedda it may be that Germanus was a Roman grafted into a British pedigree.

Urien's descent from March, son of Meirchion, from Boneddy y Gwyr Godledd:

Vryen m. Kynuarch m. Meirchawn m. Gorust Letlwm m. Keneu m. Coel

Vortigern and Ambrosius the Elder
If Coel's title was Guotepauc (in Latin Vortiporus) then Vortigern may have meant something similar – along the lines of High King. Vortigern emerged one generation after Coel. There is thought to have been two Vortigerns, which I will discuss later.

The first writer to tell the story of Vortigern was the 6th-century historian Gildas, writing his De Excidio et Conquestu Britanniae (Latin: "On the Ruin and Conquest of Britain") in the first decades of the 6th century. He tells us how "all the councillors, together with that proud usurper [omnes consiliarii una cum su- perbo tyranno]" made the mistake of inviting "the fierce and impious Saxons" to settle in Britain.

According to Gildas, apparently a small group came at first, and was settled "on the eastern side of the island, by the invitation of the unlucky (infaustus) usurper". This small group invited more of their countrymen to join them, and the colony grew. Eventually the Saxons demanded that "their monthly allotments" be increased, and when their demands were eventually refused, broke their treaty and plundered the lands of the Romano-British.

Gildas never addresses Vortigern as the king of Britain. He is termed an usurper (tyrannus), but not solely responsible for inviting the Saxons. To the contrary, he is supported/supporting a "Council", which may be a government based on the representatives of all the "cities" (citivates) or a part thereof.

Gildas also does not see Vortigern as bad; he just qualifies him as "unlucky" (infaustus) and lacking judgement, which is understandable, as these mercenaries proved to be faithless.

The first to consider Gildas' account was Bede, who is highly praised by modern scholars for his scholarship and analysis. This, however, has hardly any bearing on his description of the 5th and 6th centuries, because Bede, writing in the early- to mid-8th century, mostly paraphrases Gildas's writings in his Historia Ecclesiastica Gentis Anglorum and De Temporum Ratione.

Bede only adds several details, perhaps most importantly the name of this "proud tyrant", Vortigern (Latin Uurtigernus, Uuertigernus or Vertigernus, from the Old Welsh Gwrtheyrn. The Old English version was Wyrtgeorn).

Bede gives names to the leaders of the Saxons, Hengest and Horsa; and specifically identifies their tribes, the Saxons, Angles, and Jutes.

The Historia Brittonum (History of the Britons), usually attributed to Nennius, a monk from Bangor, Gwynedd in Wales, was probably compiled during the early 9th century. The writer mentions a great number of sources, ranging from dry chronicles to scurrilous libel.

"Nennius" was the first to blacken the name of Vortigern, who nonetheless figures heavily in genealogies of many Welsh royal houses. Vortigern The Elder was opposed by a Romanised general named Ambrosius (the Elder).

Nennius gives us the dates of 425 for when Vortigern came to power, the date of 428 of the arrival of the Saxons (Adventus Saxonum) and 437 for the battle between Vitalinus (Vortigern the Elder) with Ambrosius The Elder at the Battle of Wallop (probably in Hampshire). Later legends give Vortigern a wife called Severa, who was the daughter of rebel emperor Magnus Maximus.

Ambrosius, as an opposing chieftain, may have used the title Gwledig (guletic). Therefore I believe is found in the Welsh histories as Amlach. His son was Brychan ap Amlach Gwledig, who I would suggest is remembered in mythology as "Amlawdd Gwledig."

An interesting counter-theory is that Ambrosius the Elder was the Irish-Dyfed king Aed Brose which certainly sounds like Ambrose but it seems unlikely an Irishman would be so romanised. Amlach was the son of Tudwal and Gratiana (daughter of Magnus Maximus) and Vortigern married Severa, Gratiana's sister. Vortigern would therefore be Ambrosius' uncle by marriage. Ambrosius married his cousin Ribwast (Vortigern's daughter) and their son was Brychan ap Amlach.

Lineage:

Nonn mam Dewi oed verch y Anna verch Vthyr pendragon. Mam Anna oed verch Eigyr (verch) Anlawd wledic.

Nonn, mother of David, was the daughter of Anna d. of Uther Pendragon. [Her] mother Anna was the daughter of Eigyr daughter of Lord Anlawd.

Constans and Ceneu

According to legend, the last Roman ruler of Britain was Constantine ap Solomon, no doubt based on Constantine III. In legend, Constantine was succeeded by his eldest son Constans the monk, who was overthrown by Vortigern the Younger and he by Ambrosius the Younger (Ambrosius Aurelianus).

British legend, aided by Geoffrey of Monmouth, states that Constans was elected by the Britons as king after Constantine's death. This contradicts the known history of Constans, as does the remainder of his British story. The legend claims Constans, older brother to Ambrosius Aurelianus and Uther Pendragon, spent his early life studying at a monastery. However this Constantine and Constans lived a generation or two too early to have been the father of any Uther or Ambrosius Aurelianus.

The Succession

> Emperor Constantine
> Constans
> Vortigern the Elder
> Ambrosius the Elder
> Vortigern and Vortimer
> Ambrosius Aurelianus

Often it is not made clear there were two Vortigerns and Ambrosius and so the succession is recorded:

> Emperor Constantine
> Constans
> Vortigern
> Ambrosius
> Vortigern
> Ambrosius

The characters of Constantine and St Constans were most likely based on Constantine III and St Ceneu, son of Coel who ruled in the North as the Vortigern Dynasty battled for control of the South.

Ceneu may have been canonised because he upheld the old Christian ways while under intense pressure from invading pagans.

St Constans of legend and St Ceneu in history were exact contemporaries and sit perfectly in that generation between Constantine and Ambrosius. They both have the distinction of being associated with the invitation of Saxons to Britain.

High-King Vortigern's policy of employing Saxon mercenaries to defeat British enemies meant that, for most of his reign, Ceneu was obliged to accept the help of the Saxons, Octha and Ebissa, in pushing back invading Picts from his kingdom.Their interference was widely resented and it was not until after the Kentish rebellion that they were finally brought under control. Magnanimous in victory, Ceneu allowed the Saxons to settle in Deywr (Deira - East Yorkshire). Once again, the major Arthurian event is linked to Yorkshire.

Ceneu appears in Geoffrey of Monmouth's History of the Kings of Britain as having attended the coronation of the great King Arthur.

Another link to the north for Arthur - and now we have the indication that St Ceneu may have been important to his story. When Ceneu abdicated he passed his kingdom onto his three sons, Meirchionn who held Cumbria; Pabo who held the Pennines and Mar who held Ebrauc (York).

Saxon/Jute Rulers in the North

- Esa/Horssa/Octha/Osla Big Knife
- Eoppa (contemporary with Arthur)
- Ida (ruled circa 547)

Who was Emrys?

Then Aurelius led his army to York in order to besiege Octa, the son of Hengist... **Geoffrey of Monmouth**.

Ambrosius "Emrys Guletic" Aurelianus (Ambrosius the Younger), not to be confused with Ambrosius the Elder (Amlach) is a curious case because he is documented in history but not in pedigrees - it seems strange that nobody claimed descent from him.

If the legendary Constantine was rightfully succeeded by his son Ambrosius Aurelianus, who then was Ambrosius to the real Constantine, St Ceneu - of course he was his son. The identity of Ambrosius Aurelianus, Count of Britain, is found in the Welsh genealogies as Pabo Post Prydain, the 'Father and Pillar of Britain'.

This was also suggested by historians Blackett and Wilson who state:

"Pappo Post Prydain - the father and pillar of Britain - who was elected King of all Britains... This type of election was rare and only took place in times of great emergency....

"[Pappo] was one of only three Kings to be elected by the British... Pappo fills the age of Ambrosius Aurelianus."

Ambrosius meant "Divine one" or "Immortal one" – a fitting title for the Father and Pillar of Britain.

As the Pillar of Britain, he was again associated with Hadrian's Wall, but his title suggests a national leader - the Commes of Britain.

And Pabo's career did indeed spread beyond York - his final resting place was Wales and in book 2 we will discover he was known in Britanny as well. He may have ruled from Papcastle in Cumbria.

In legend the characters of the boy Emrys and Merlin Emrys become somewhat intertwined - and we will see that Pabo also shares some of the characteristics of Merlin. Of course the later Myrddin (Merlin Caledonus) is where the 'wizard' takes his name - but some of his traits are found in Pabo.

43

The Resting place of Merlin Emrys:
Llanbabo Church's own description reads:
"Llanbabo Church was established here around AD 460...

"It is thought that Pabo... was the son of a [Northern] chieftain. Pabo died on 9th November AD 530, and so this is the date of his Feast Day.

"A gravestone discovered in the graveyard of the Church sometime during the mid to late 17th Century is believed to be that of St Pabo or King Pabo, as he once was.

"This stone can now be inspected inside the church and discovered to bear the legend 'Hic Iacet Pabo Post Prud...' - 'Here Lies Pabo Post Prydein'."

"This title of 'King' is derived from two main sources. The first is the effigy on Pabo's gravestone inside the church.

"Pabo appears to be wearing a crown and holding a sceptre. These are the traditional insignia of 'Kingship'.

"Secondly, and more apparent is the legend that Pabo Post Prydein was the 'Pillar of Britain' or 'The Bulwark of Celtic Wales' against the Picts (Scottish Tribe)."

"Although his resting place is now in Llanbabo Church, in his former role as King, Pabo's kingdom was in the Pennines, in central Britain, which he defended against the said Picts.

"St Pabo turned his back on his warlike ways and travelled here to Anglesey where he founded his church."

Gwyr y Gogledd:

[D]unaut map Pappo map Ceneu map Coyl hen.

Meirionydd:
[C]atguallaun liu map Guitcun map Samuil pennissel map Pappo post Priten map Ceneu map Gyl [Coyl] hen.

Geoffrey of Monmouth muddled up the story of the "The Boy Emrys", who grew up to be the king's advisor, with the later bard Myrdinn (Merlin) and so a character of Merlin Emrys was born. However Pabo really did start life as a boy prince, then became a hermit and a saint and died an old bearded man in Wales

Pabo Post Prydain succeeded his father Ceneu as Protector of Britain, Father and Pillar of Britain.

Gildas records this:

"The remnants (of the British)...take up arms, and challenge their victors to battle under Ambrosius Aurelianus. He was a man of unassuming character, who, alone of the Roman race, chanced to survive the storm in which his parents, people un-doubtedly clad in the purple, had been killed. Their offspring in our days have greatly degenerated from their ancestral noble- ness. From that time the citizens were sometimes victorious, sometimes the enemy...up to the year of the Siege of Mons Badonicus."

Pabo Post Prydain may have had the real name Emrys, which was later romanised to Ambrosius. His title 'father and pillar of Britain' has caused some, such as Ronan Coghlan, to speculate that because his name seems to be Pabo his Romanised name would have been Pompey.

Pabo, or Ambrosius, was born in about 450 and crowned quite young - say at 15 years old. Ceneu installed him as King of the Pennines while his brother Mar was given Ebrauc (York).

As Ambrosius' reign began to grow, he not only fought Hengist, Esa and Octha in the North. he would have been an adversary of the Saxon King who is the patriarch of the Sussex kingship - Ælle, a man who also considered himself King of Britain - or Bretwalda.

Ælle is recorded in early sources as the first king of the South Saxons, reigning in what is now called Sussex, England, from 477. Ælle and three of his sons are reported to have arrived from the continent near what is now Selsey Bill - the exact location is under the sea, and is probably a sandbank currently known as the Owers - and fought with the Britons.

A victory in 491 at present day Pevensey is said to have ended with the Saxons slaughtering their opponents to the last man. Ælle is recorded as being the first bretwalda, or "Britain-ruler" and Bede stated that his rule stretched all the way to the Humber.

In Arthurian legends, Ambrosius Aurelianus was succeeded by his brother Uther. In reality the real Ambrosius Aurelianus, pillar of Britain, was succeeded by his brother Mar.

If the Arthurian character of Uther Pendragon is the equivalent of the historic king Mar, we need to examine if the two share any traits and how the name Mar came to morph into Uther - we will see it did exactly that and Mar was indeed the prototype Uther Pendragon.

Uther Pendragon

The first mythical mentions of Uther are short mentions in Welsh poetry. In the 'Dialogue of Arthur and the Eagle' (Ymddiddan Arthur a'r Eryr), a work drawing on traditions earlier than Geoffrey of Monmouth, the eponymous eagle reveals himself as Arthur's deceased nephew Eliwlat vab Madawc vab Uthyr (this genealogy is repeated in the mid-15th-century Pedwar Marchog ar Hugain Llys Arthur).

If Arthur was indeed the son of Uthyr, then he and Madawg were brothers. This Madog, son of Uthyr, is known from another pre-Geoffrey text, Madawg drut ac Erof in the Book of Taliesin:

Madog, the rampart of rejoicing. Madog, before he was in the grave, he was a fortress of generosity [consisting] of feat(s) and play. The son of Uthyr, before death he handed over pledges.

In the early poem "Pa gur" from the Black Book of Carmarthen, one of Arthur's band of men is named as: *Mabon son of Myrdon, Uthr Pendragon's servant.*

A common question is whether Uther was viewed as Arthur's father previous to Geoffrey of Monmouth's histories. The answer, it seems, is yes.

In the 'Dialogue of Arthur and the Eagle', the eagle reveals itself to be Arthur's deceased nephew, Eliwlod son of Madawg son of Uthyr (stanzas 7-9), i.e. Arthur and Madog are both sons of Uthyr.

In addition to this, in the Book of Taliesin poem Marwnat vthyr pen Uthyr says:

"I have shared my refuge, a ninth share in Arthur's valour", and later that "The world would not exist if it were not for my progeny" indicating he has passed on his qualities (or his kingdom) to Arthur.

Therefore, from Welsh mythology, there is nothing to suggest Uther was not Arthur's father and compelling evidence that he was.

Following these brief but significant mentions in Welsh mythology, Uther's story is first told in full by Geoffrey of Monmouth in his "History of Kings of Britain". As one of the two younger brothers of the murdered King Constans, he apparently fled, at a young age, to the Royal Court of his cousin, King Budic. As a young man, Uther returned to Britain with his elder brother, Ambrosius, and together they fought for their ancestral rights, eventually defeating the usurping Vortigern and placing Ambrosius on the throne.

Throughout Ambrosius' reign, Uther was his brother's staunchest ally. He commanded the King's forces in Ireland. A dragon-shaped comet appeared in the sky at the time of his brother's death. But Uther's adventures do not all taken place in the south - on the contrary, he would seem very much based in the north.

Most of his reign was taken up with campaigning against Saxon and Irish invaders in the North of Britain, where he held court at what would later be Pendragon Castle in Westmorland. He was, at first, unsuccessful against the Angles of Bernicia. Osla, and the Jutish Octa (unless Osla and Octa were identical), defeated Uther's armies at York (Caer-Ebrauc). However, he soon turned the tables at the ensuing Battle of Mount Damen. Uther later travelled even further north to help the Kings of Strathclyde pacify the Scots.

In identifying Uther Pendragon, we are looking for the man who succeeded his brother Ambrosius, a man who fought invaders in the North of Britain, whose castle was in Westmorland, and who fought in Yorkshire and Strathclyde. Of course the perfect candidate is the real brother of Ambrosius Aurelianus - King Mar (Mor) of Westmorland.

Uther was the mythological brother of Ambrosius who ruled York in the late 400s, Mar was the historical brother who did so at the same time. But why would King Mar be remembered as Uther? The answer is simple - Uther or Iubher is written using the same Ogham 'yew tree' symbol as Ebrauc (York), therefore Uther Pendragon is the Pendragon of York. Uther's name was recorded as Iubher and this shows that his name, much like his exploits, was derived from his hometown of York.

In his book, Arthur and the Lost Kingdoms, Moffat writes:

"Petillus Cerialis marched the 9th Legion North from Lincoln to a place they called Eboracum, or York, or Ebor as the Anglican Archbishop still styles himself. It comes from the Celtic for Yew tree, Iubhar which, because of the traditional use of its elastic branches, came by extension to mean bowmen."

The Illustrated Encyclopaedia of Arthurian Legends (Coghlan) states: "Iubhar (the Irish name for Arthur's father) was actually a mistranslation of Uther."

This could not be any clearer: Iubhar = York
                                    Iubher = Uther

So Uther just meant York - and who better to take that title than the 5th century King of Ebrauc, Mar. As for Mar, here is a man who fought across the sea. His nickname Mor is Welsh for Sea. He is Pendragon of York and King of the Sea! He is Mor of Morland.

In pedigrees, he is variously called Mor, Mar or Masguid Gloff (Masguid the Lame), a name which, roughly translated, might have meant his Roman title was Maximus Claudius. If he ruled the York area he probably also held court at the Roman base of Campuduno - now known as Leeds. Pendragon Castle stands just off the B3259, four miles south of Kirkby Stephen in Westmorland - there's that name Mor again. Pendragon Castle is, naturally, said to be named after King Uther Pendragon who supposedly built the place as one of his northern strongholds.

An old local rhyming couplet tells how he tried to divert the River Eden for use as a moat:

Let Uther Pendragon do what he can, Eden will run where Eden ran

Of course as well as being a great leader of battles there are two other things Uther Pendragon was famous for: Seducing the beautiful Igraine, wife of Gorlois and becoming the father of King Arthur.

Pendragon Castle ruins

In Geoffrey of Monmouth's Historia Regum Britanniae, Igerna enters the story as the wife of Gorlois, Duke of Cornwall. King Uther Pendragon falls in love with her and attempts to force his attentions on her at his court. She informs her husband, who departs with her to Cornwall without asking leave. This sudden departure gives Uther Pendragon an excuse to make war on Gorlois. Gorlois conducts the war from the castle of Dimilioc but places his wife in safety in the castle of Tintagel.

Disguised as Gorlois by Merlin's sorcery, Uther Pendragon is able to enter Tintagel to satisfy his lust. He manages to rape Igraine by deceit - she believes that she is lying with her husband and becomes pregnant with Arthur. Her husband Gorlois dies in battle that same night. Geoffrey does not say, and later accounts disagree, as to whether Gorlois died before or after Arthur was begotten (something that might be important in determining whether or not a child could be made legitimate by a later marriage to its true father). Uther Pendragon later marries Igraine.

So if Constans is Ceneu, Ambrosius is Pabo and Uther is Mar... Who is Uther's son Arthur? That would of course be... Mar's son Arthwys!

Unfortunately, the later legends treat Uther as a southern King and Gorlois and Igraine as King and Queen of Dumnonia/Kernow (roughly Devon/Cornwall) unfortunately no such names exist in the pedigrees of Dumnonian kingship. This has caused some to reason that Uther, Igraine and Gorlois were fictional. Of course they were not, the 'experts' were just looking at the wrong end of the country!

Just as King Arthur's mother was Igraine (Irish Grainne - maiden) daughter of Amlawdd Gwledig, the real Arthur's mother was Gwenllian ('maiden in white linen') daughter of the real Amlawdd, (Brychan ap Amlach Gwledig).

The mythical Igraine as the wife of Gorlois, In Gwenllian's immediate viscinity when at least two kings called Gorlais - she may well have been married to a historic northern king called Gorlais. There are a few kings called Gorlais in the king lists and they are all without exception found in the north.

It is clear that Geoffrey did not invent the Uther-Igraine-Gorlois deception as the Welsh Triads state that Uthyr was a great and renowned enchanter/magician who teaches one of the "Three Great Enchantments of the Island of Britain" to Menw, son of Teirgwaedd, a character who is one of Arthur's men and has the ability to shape-shift (as Uther did to seduce Igraine) and to become invisible in Culhwch ac Olwen.

Mar as Uther, Gwenllian and Igraine and Gorlais as Gorlois are well established in the York area, along with Mar's brother Pabo Post Prydain. Very simply, if you were to travel back in time to 470, you would find that the two brothers who succeeded Constantine and defended York were the proverbial Uther and Emrys - they were Mar and Pabo. And of course this Uther had a son called Arthwys.

Again, if you were to build a time machine and go back to 500AD, the only ruler with a name anything like Arthur was Arthwys ap Mar - he was in the right place at the right time.

Mar in the Triads

Once again this shows Mar was connected with Madog:

The grave of the three serene persons on an elevated hill,
In the valley of Gwynn Gwynionawg--
Mor, and Meilyr, and Madawg.

The grave of Madawg, the splendid bulwark
In the meeting of contention, the grandson of Urien,
The best son to Gwyn of Gwynlliwg.

The grave of Mor, the magnificent, immovable sovereign,
The foremost pillar in the conflict,
The son of Peredur Penwedig

Who Was the Real King Arthur?

In Arthur, courage was closely linked with generosity, and he made up his mind to harry the Saxon... He therefore called together all the young men whom I have just mentioned and marched on York... **Geoffrey of Monmouth**

Arthwys ap Mar as King Arthur

In mythology, Constans was followed by Emrys and Uther, and they by Arthur. In real history Ceneu was followed by Pabo and Mar and they by Arthur. Arthur was the son of Mar (Uther) and the nephew of Pabo (Emrys) and the grandson of Ceneu (Constans) and great grandson of Coel Hen. And, like his ancestors, he ruled from York to Hadrian's Wall and down across the sprawling Peennines. In the Welsh Triads his Kingdom was called Pen Rhionydd, he was also called the King of Pen Y Ghent. Today he is remembered by historians as "Arthwys of the Pennines" or "Arthwys of Elmet." Mythology remembers him as Arthur Pendragon of Camelot and the Round Table. He should be remembered as King Arthur, Dux Bellorum, defender of Camulod, champion of Badon and Camboglanna.

The earliest written reference to Arthur (Aneirin's Gododdin) is set in the North Yorkshire area. The bard Taliesin also places him in the north, around Hadrian's Wall. The name itself - Arthur - may be related to Artorius, who - Lucius Artorius Castus - was a commander garrisoned on Hadrian's Wall a few hundred years prior to Arthur. Nennius calls Arthur the Dux of Britain, a title used by Romans in defence of the area around Hadrian's Wall. Nennius lists 12 battles for Arthur, some of which are easier to identify than others. They include:

- The River Glein
- The River Dubglas
- The River Dubglas
- The River Dubglas
- The River Dubglas
- The River Bassas
- Forest of Celidon
- Fort Guinnion
- City of the Legion
- River Tribruit
- Mount Agned
- Badon Hill

The Annales Cambrae lists Arthur fighting at Badon and dying at Camlan - most likely Camboglanna on Hadrian's Wall. Therefore all the evidence starts to point towards Arthur stationed around York and Hadrian's Wall, and fighting the Angles in the East and the Picts in the North.

Even later legends have Arthur fighting these campaigns - Geoffrey of Monmouth has him besieging York and then heading to Scotland. We can then look at the pedigrees of the kings' ancestry. There is an Athrwys in Gwynedd who lived too late to be Arthur. There is an Artur in Scotland and an Artuir in Dyfed who were closer but still too late. But then there is an Arthwys in the Yorkshire area who is of precisely the right age.

Arthwys ap Mar of Elmet, Ebrauc and the Pennines is precusely the right age and location to be Arthur. He was about 40 when Arthur would have fought his 12th battle and around 60 when Arthur would have died. He ruled the area known as Dux, that Arthur was said to have ruled.

But there is so much more to it and this. I have identified no less than FIFTY Arthurian characters including Merlin, Guinevere, Lancelot and Mordred who can all be found in the immediate and extended family of this historic king.

Upon reading this book there should be little doubt that King Arthur was actually King Arthwys.

Arthwys vs Arthur vs Artur vs Arthuis

At this point some readers may point out the difference between the spelling of the name. To answer this, I would like to use my own Irish surname as an example of how spellings vary over the years. My ancestor was Aedhagain. The surname became Mhic Aedhagain, then MacAodhagain, then MacKeighan, then variations like MacEgan, McKeegan and Kegan appeared. My great great great grandfather was recorded in a census as John Kegan (which was then recorded online as John Regan), but his son's marriage certificate called him John Keegan. And these eight or so spellings are just over the last 800 years - with Arthur we are talking about the last 1500 years. Again in the Welsh side of my family Hendwr became Hendower and again as Hender.

Something I learned very early on when researching my family tree was not to look only for precise spellings. When going back 1500 years there is bound to be different dialects.

In other words, the spelling need not be "Arthur" for the man to be Arthur. Another example is Guinever, Gwenhwyfar and Guanhumara. Another is Maelgwyn, Malgo, Magloconus, Melkin etc.

Arthur is recorded as a man of the north in the Bonnedd y Gwyr Gogledd.

Bonedd y Gwyr Gogledd:

Clydno Eidin & Chynan Genhir & Chynuelyn Drwsgyl, Kynvawr Hadgaddvc & Chatrawt Calchuynyd, meibon Kynnwyt Kynnwydyon m. Kynuelyn m. Arthwys m. Mar m. Keneu m. Cole

Gwrgi & Phered meibon Eliffer Gosgord Uawr m. Arthwys m. Mar m. Keneu m. Coel

Gwendoleu & Nud & Chof meibyon Keidyaw m. Arthwys m. Mar m. Keneu m. Coel

Here we see that Arthur, like Mark, was descended from Coel. This is the original of Arthur's supposed Cornish pedigree.

Arthur is exactly what we expected - the Northern Dux in descent from Coel Hen, garrisoned at Hadrian's Wall and, like Constantine, crowned in York.

Arthur Pendragon

No historical man was ever listed as Arthur Pendragon - however Arthwys ap Mar comes very close. In one manuscript he is referred to as Arthur Penuchel (Arthur High Head) or Ben Uchel - confirming he was indeed known as Arthur. The lineage shows him being succeeded by his grandson Peredur:

Gwrgi a pheredur ac arthur penuchel a tonlut a hortnan a dyrnell trydyth gwyn dorliud.

Family tree of the legendary Arthur in the Brut:

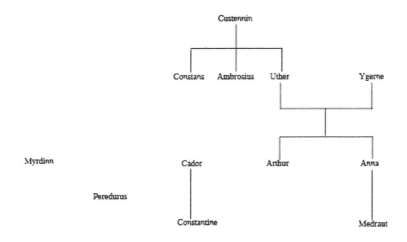

Compare to family tree of Arthwys ap Mor:

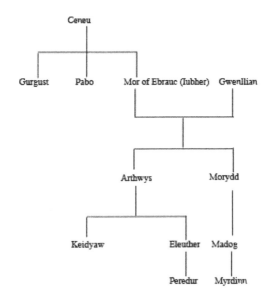

The life of Arthur

In 470AD Arthur ap Mar was born. His father was the most powerful King in Britain and his mother Gwenllian was the daughter of another of the most powerful leaders, Brychan.

Arthur's uncle, Ambrosius Aurelianus, known to the Britons as Pabo Post Prydain (Father and Pillar of Britain) was still the figurehead and cast a formidable shadow.

When we first meet the baby Arthur in the legends he is taken from his mother by Merlin – otherwise known as Merlin Emrys.

And so we have two versions of the Emrys story. We have him as Emrys brother of Uther, a wise diplomat and we have him as Merlin Emrys, a fortune telling advisor to the king. The real name of Ambrosius was Emrys and so now it becomes clear. Emrys was really Arthur's uncle Ambrosius Aurelianus.

Just as the mythological Arthur was taken from his mother by a king-making "wizard", the real Arthur was taken by someone no less powerful – the father and pillar of Britain himself. Who better to school Arthur in the ways of being a king than the previous king himself?

Arthur ap Mar and his heritage is shown in the Celtic genealogies:

Bonedd Gwŷr y Gogledd

Chatravt Calchuynyd meibon Kynnvyt Kynnvydyon m Kynue- lyn m Arthwys m Mar m Keneu

Gwendoleu a Nud a Chof meibyon Keidyav m Arthwys m Mar m Keneu m Coel

Arthur was the son of Mar ap Ceneu ap Coel and the father of Keidyaw and Cynvelyn. From names alone we can see characters emerging.

In Ambrosius Aurelianus (Merlin Emrys) we see a civilised man. One who respects the Roman ways, and according to Gildas, wore the purple robes of office. A statesman, a wise leader, one who was called not only the pillar of Britain – but the father of Britain. No wonder he took Arthur to raise as his own!

In King Mar we see a rougher war leader. His nickname "Uther Pendragon" means "terrible head dragon" his other names Mor and Gloff suggested a wounded warrior fighting battles at land and at sea. A man who would seduce his enemy's wife. A man who was not the "pillar" of Britain, but the Dragon of Britain.

Arthur's name means Bear. The name suggests strength, but also quietness and softness. Maybe already we can see some of Arthur's character. As Artorius he took after Ambrosius as a quiet statesman of Britain. As Arthur map Uther he was the Bear son of the Dragon, a warlord who would crush his enemies with one swipe of his paw.

Make no mistake. The young Arthur was bred for war and bred to lead the country.

From Artorius to Arthwys

Arthur had another legacy to uphold. Arthur was descended from northern Britain's greatest Roman soldier. He was descended from Lucius Artorius Castus and bore the name Artorius or Arthur in his honour.

Lucius Artorius Castus was a military commander of ancient Rome, suggested by some as the historical basis for King Arthur - but he was actually the man's ancestor.

What is known of Artorius comes from inscriptions on fragments of a sarcophagus, and a memorial plaque, both found in Podstrana on the Dalmatian coast. Although undated, the likely time period of the sarcophagus (before 200), combined with the inscription's mention of Artorius being a dux, suggests that he was the unnamed commander of a 185 expedition to Armorica mentioned by Herodian.

According to the inscription, Artorius was a centurion of the Legio III Gallica, then moved to VI Ferrata, then to V Macedonica, where he was promoted to primus pilus.

He was then made praepositus of the classis Misenensis (the Bay of Naples fleet), followed by a position as praefectus of the VI Victrix which was based in Britain from 122AD. Artorius likely participated in the guarding of Hadrian's Wall.

When VI Victrix mutinied, Artorius seems to have remained loyal, since Pertinax soon after promoted him to dux and sent him to Armorica with several cohorts of cavalry, where he was successful in suppressing an uprising. Artorius then retired from the army and became procurator centenaris (governor) of Liburnia, a part of Dalmatia.

Lucius Artorius Castus led an elite unit in Britain. The cavalry was thought to be made up of heavy Sarmatian horsemen. The Sarmatians told a story about a mythical hero called Batraz which may have been handed down the generations and inspired his descendant Arthur.

The Sarmatians shared an almost spiritual connection with their weapons, and so the life of Batraz revolves around his magic sword. While a young man, Batraz pulls his sword from the roots of a tree.

Legend has it that Batraz tells his friend to throw his sword into the ocean. The warrior is reluctant at first, not only because of the quality of the sword but because of the spiritual connection it had with Batraz. But in the end the warrior did throw the sword and it was caught by a water goddess.

Lucius Artorius is remembered in Celtic legends as 'Good King Lucius' (Lleifer Mawr). Arthur is descended from Artorius on his mother and father's side.

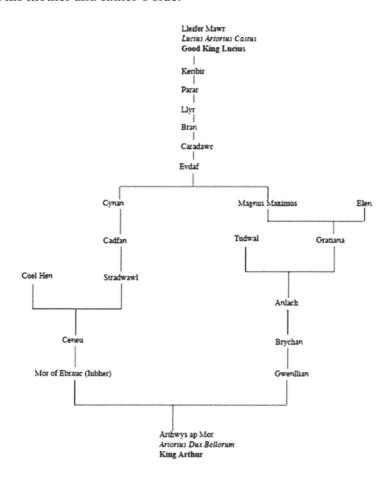

The Ladies of Avalon
In the Arthurian romances, Arthur is related to a host of holy priestesses.

THE LADY OF THE LAKE
TELLETH ARTHVR OF THE
SWORD EXCALIBVR

Igraine: Arthur's mother. The daughter of Amlawdd Gwledig. She is also the mother of Morgan Le Fey.

Nimue: Otherwise known as Niniane or Vivianne. She was an enchantress who fell in love with Merlin and became the famous Lady in the Lake.

Morgan Le Fay and Anna: Alternatively Morgana and Morgause. Morgan and her sister are often combined in legends. Morgan was jealous of her half brother Arthur, sometimes because King Uther (Arthur's father) killed Gorlois (Morgan's father). She sometimes takes some of Nimue's attributes and is an antagonist towards Merlin.

Having identified Arthwys ap Mar as the King Arthur of legend, we have already identified St Gwenlian (daughter of Brychan ap Amlach) with Igraine (daughter of Amlawdd), so where can we find likely contenders for Ninian, Morgan and Anna? Well - right in the family tree of Arthwys ap Mar! Gwenllian's sister was Saint Nyfain – the real Niniane.

Gwenllian's mother Ribwast was said to be the sister of Vortimer (son of Vortigern) and Vortimer's daughters were St Madrun and St Anna – the real Morgan and Anna.

For Gwenllian, her sister Nyfain and their cousins Madrun and Anna to be regarded as saints they must have been extremely spiritual women.

Let's compare these priestesses with their mythological counterparts:

Mythology & History

Igraine mother of Arthur ~ Gwenllian mother of Arthwys
Niniane ~ Nyfain
Morgan ~ Madrun
Anna ~ Anna

These priestesses must have had an influence on the young Arthur. From his family tree alone we can see the true character of our King Arthur. On his paternal side were warlords like Coel, Ceneu, Mar and Pabo, high kings of Northern Britain, ruling from the old Roman capital of Ebrauc (York), on his mother's side were priestesses who later became known as Saints like Gwenllian, Nyfain, Madrun and Anna.

The coronation of Arthur

According to legend, King Arthur was crowned at age 15, which would have been around 485. According to Geoffrey of Monmouth the coronation was well attended by other royalty, and of course some were related to the real King Arthur, Arthur of the Pennines. In addition to these great leaders there came other famous men of equal importance: Dunaut map Papo, Cheneus map Coil...

Papo is of course Pabo Post Prydain (Ambrosius) and Cheneus map Coil is of course Ceneu ap Coel, the grandfather of Arthur. Geoffrey of Monmouth actually lists Arthwys ap Mar's uncle and grandfather as attending the coronation - what other Arthur could they be referring to?

When he was a child, Arthur's uncle, Ambrosius Aurelianus, the father and Pillar of Britain and Arthur's father Mar, the Pendragon of York, battled Ælle's Saxons. Now, at the age of 15, Arthur was crowned king at Ebrauc.

Once again, the Arthurian tale remains firmly rooted in York. So, if Arthur was king, where was his court and who was in it?

PENNINE DRAGON

Family tree of the mythological King Arthur from Welsh sources:

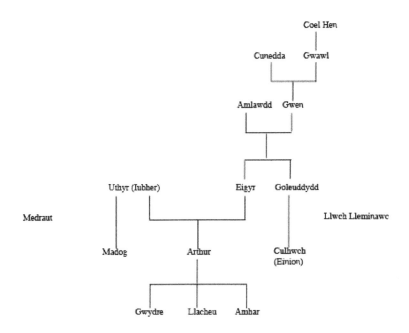

Family tree of Arthwys ap Mar to contrast with Welsh sources:

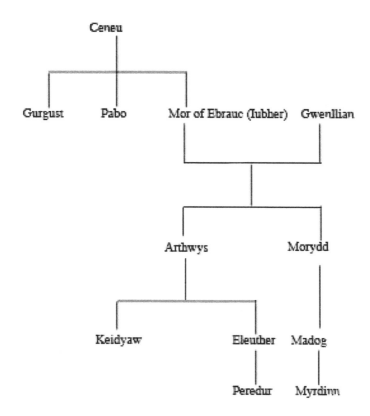

Here we see the tree of Arthwys includes:

Mor (Uther)
Gwenllian (Eigyr)
Arthwys (Arthur)
Morydd (Mordred)
Keidyaw (Cador)
Myrddin (Merlin)
Peredur (Perceval)

The Real Camelot

Camelot is only introduced as Arthur's castle in later medieval romances, but there would seem to be a grain of truth in the name – and that grain comes from the fact that Camulod or variations of it were used for at least two sites by Roman legions – the most documented being Camulodonum (Colchester) home of the Catuvellauni tribe at the time of the Roman conquest. But Colchester is a long way from York.

Arthur's father Mar was the King of York (Ebrauc) - he even took the name Uther (Iubher) meaning York. Therefore we should not be surprised to find Arthur's legendary castle nearby. For years scholars have suggested that Camelot was originally called Camulodonum - but the only snag is that Camulodonum was the old Roman name for Colchester, a place never associated with Arthur.

But consider the name Colchester (Coel's castle) - where else would you expect the legendary Coel, Arthur's great grandfather to have a castle but in the north. And sure enough, there was another place called Camulodonum by the Romans.

The settlement at Slack, near Huddersfield, may have its origins in the impressive Iron Age hillfort of Almondbury, only five miles away. Like modern Colchester, the Romans established a small military fort there and named it Camulodunum after the ancient Celtic War-God, Camulos.

So let's go back to our premise. Geoffrey of Monmouth tells us that Uther Pendragon who succeeded his brother defended York and then his son Arthur was crowned in a ceremony attended by Pabo and Ceneu. We later learn from the likes of Chretien de Troyes that Arthur's base was Camelot.

In reality we have Mar (Uther/Iubher) succeeding his brother and defending York, and then his son Arthwys being crowned in a ceremony attended by his uncle Pabo and grandfather Ceneu. And in his very kingdom was Camulod.

In the early second century AD, Ptolemy, in his famed treatise on Geographia listed as the last of his nine poleis attributed to the

Brigantes tribe of northern Britain, following the base of the Sixth Legion at Eboracum/York, a place named Camulodunum, evidently somewhere in northern England.

The Antonine Itinerary, produced in the mid-second century, contains within the second road route in Britain, Iter II, a place named Camboduno somewhere in the West Riding of Yorkshire, some 9 miles from Calcaria (Tadcaster, North Yorkshire) and 20 miles from Mamucio (Manchester).

The next major geographical work is the 7th century Ravenna Cosmology, where appears a place named Camulodono, listed between the entries for Alunna (Watercrook, Lancashire) and Calunio (Lancaster, Lancashire).

This fort measures 256 feet square (78 m2) within the defences giving an occupation area of just 11/2 acres (0.6 ha). It was defended by a 20 foot wide turf rampart, the outer wall of which was laid upon foundations of stone.

The fort was built during the Flavian period, probably c.AD80, the first buildings, including the gates, were of timber construction. The buildings were later part-replaced by stone, but the fort appears to have been abandoned before the work was complete, possibly because the auxiliary garrison had been moved to the northern frontier.

The fort was partially reconstructed during the first quarter of the second century, when its internal buildings were replaced in stone. The original Flavian fort was occupied until the late-second or early-third centuries, as attested by pottery from the times of Hadrian and Antonine.

Within the real King Arthur's kingdom was a fortress called Camulodunum - surely proof that we have identified King Arthur of Camelot.

Until recently Slack was thought to be a fairly minor Roman fort abandoned in the third century but new evidence has come to light that it was once a magnificent fortress, with giant amphitheatre and water spring, and was occupied until Arthur's times.

Arthur's Camulod really was as grand as the legends say. Archaelogists in nearby Huddersfield believe crowds of up to

2,000 would pack into the amphitheatre to watch horsemanship displays by the Roman cavalry.

Granville Clay, project co-ordinator for the Huddersfield and District Archaeological Society, said: "It is a very exciting find. We had studied an old map dating from 1854 which (calling the fort Campodunum) had a circle marked on it and the words 'Circus here'.

"It means that the Slack fort was probably far more important in Roman history than people have previously believed.

"Roman forts had paved areas outside the walls where soldiers could exercise and train for battle.

"Some cavalry forts had an enclosed circus area where horses could be trained and sometimes raced for the entertainment of the garrison and this is what we have found. Horse racing and chariot racing was common throughout the Roman Empire."

The one found at Outlane is about 80 metres in diameter but the exact shape is not known because New Hey Road cuts right through the middle of it and much of it has been built over.

Mr Clay said: "People have heard of the Circus Maximus in Rome, but many of the forts had their own circus, or amphitheatre.

"This one is quite big and I would estimate up to 2,000 people could be there to watch the horse shows.

"People have previously thought the fort was abandoned when the garrison left, but we now have evidence that it was in use for much, much longer, with people living there to look after travellers using the Roman road through Slack and to maintain the road itself."

The Society has carried out excavations at Slack to discover more about the water supply to the Roman fort and any evidence of how long the Roman road was in use after the fort was no longer used by the army.

Following the highly successful Society dig in 2007, which uncovered the aqueduct system supplying water to the fort and produced dating evidence that pointed to Romano-British activity on the site long after the supposed abandonment of the fort, members were keen to see what else might be discovered in the vicus to the north of the fort.

Throughout both trenches large areas of 'paving' were found. These may be bases for working areas, and may have been covered by wooden structures built on horizontal wooden beams. No confirmatory evidence for this was found. In both trenches there was evidence of cooking using small fireplaces, and in one of the trenches a quantity of bone was found near to two large urns and a roof tile with the stamp of the cohort which had occupied the fort.

Huddersfield and District Archaeological Society now believe that there was an active military and civilian settlement at Slack for at least another 200 years.

In other words, the Romans were in Huddersfield for most of the 400 years of their British occupation – right up until Arthur's reign as he, like his father, grandfather and great grandfather defended the land from York to Hadrian's Wall.

Very simply, when Arthwys was crowned, his kingdom included a grand palace called Camulod, the grandest in the country. How could this not be Arthur's Camelot?

Artefacts uncovered during the Archaeological Society's digs at Slack and the original Roman road have challenge the accepted theories of the Romans' short occupation in the area.

And just as Mor's name was remembered in Westmorland near the famous Pendragon Castle of Uther, so too is Arthur's name remembered as Arthuriburgum - nearby Etterby.

Etterby, in the parish of Stanwix, was called Arthur's burg, according to Joseph Nicolson and Richard Burn's History and Antiquities of the County of Westmorland and Cumberland, (Vol. 2, 1977, p. 454.)

"Etterby in old writings is called Arthuriburgum, which seems to imply that it had been a considerable village. Some affirm that it took its name from Arthur king of the Britons."

We now have Arthur, Uther, Igraine, Merlin Emrys, Amlawdd Gwledig, Constans, Morgan, Nimue and Anna all within the same dynasty of York - and central to their kingdom was Camulod.

Arthur Duke of Brittain

"The Saxons grew strong by virtue of their large number and increased in power in Britain. Hengist having died, however, his son Octha crossed from the northern part of Britain to the kingdom of Kent and from him are descended the kings of Kent.

"Then Arthur, along with the kings of Britain, fought against them in those days, but Arthur himself was the Dux Bellorum.

"His first battle was at the mouth of the river which is called Glein. His second, third, fourth, and fifth battles were above another river which is called Dubglas and is in the region of Linnuis. The sixth battle was above the river which is called Bassas. The seventh battle was in the forest of Celidon, that is Cat Coit Celidon. The eighth battle was at the fortress of Guinnion, in which Arthur carried the image of holy Mary ever virgin on his shoulders; and the pagans were put to flight on that day. And through the power of our Lord Jesus Christ, and through the power of the blessed Virgin Mary his mother, there was great slaughter among them.

"The ninth battle was waged in the City of the Legion. The tenth battle was waged on the banks of a river which is called Tribruit. The eleventh battle was fought on the mountain which is called Agnet. The twelfth battle was on Mount Badon in which there fell in one day 960 men from one charge by Arthur; and no one struck them down except Arthur himself, and in all the wars he emerged as victor.

"And while they were being defeated in all the battles, they were seeking assistance from Germany and their numbers were being augmented many times over without interruption. And they brought over kings from Germany that they might reign over them in Britain, right down to the time in which Ida reigned, who was son of Eobba. He was the first king in Bernicia, i.e., in Berneich." **Nennius C800AD**

The Welsh historian, Nennius, records twelve great victories in battle during Arthur's time as a warleader. Right after the Arthur paragraphs he tells us Ida was the next leader in Northumbria. Not only are all of Arthur's battle sites best found in the north, but so is he placed there chronologically.

The first battle was at the mouth of the river called Glein

This has been tentatively identified as one of the two Rivers Glen in Britain today, one in Lincolnshire and one in Northumberland. Unfortunately, Glen stems from the Celtic for "pure", so there were probably many rivers thus named in 6th century Britain. A battle at the former would have presumably been against the first Bernician settlers and at the latter against the northward moving East Anglians. Either could be attributed to King Arthwys. It seems most likely that Glen was Northumberland.

The second, the third, the fourth and the fifth were on another river, called the Dubglas, which is in the region of Linnuis.

The River Dubglas is modern Douglas, meaning "black water". The 2nd century geographer, Ptolemy, recorded the associated name of Lindum at the Roman Fort of Drumquhassle in the Lennox area of Scotland. The River Douglas still runs into the nearby Loch Lomond, on the borders of Strathclyde.

The better known Roman Lindum, however, is now the city of Lincoln. The surrounding area would be Linnuis: it is still called Lindsey today. Unfortunately, there is no longer a River Blackwater or the like here, but one of the waterways flowing off the muddy peat moors could easily have been originally described as such.

Geoffrey of Monmouth indicates this as the correct identification. His chronicle relates how immediately Arthur came to the throne, he swore to rid Britain of the Saxon menace and so set out to attack the Anglian stronghold at York. Hearing of this, the Deiran leader, Colgrin, gathered together an alliance of Saxons, Scots and Picts and marched south to meet him. They clashed on the River Douglas. Geoffrey also describes an ensuing

Battle of Lincoln, probably one of the successive battles on the same river, thus identifying it as the Witham.

There is also the River Douglas near where I grew up in Wigan in Lancashire which was on an important Roman road. Wigan was called Coccium. The Douglas flows through Wigan and Linnuis may be Lancs.

After winning five battles, Arthur's reputation as a warleader in Britain must have been growing considerably.

The River Douglas in Wigan

The sixth battle was on the river called Bassas

Only one convincing possible identification appears to have been forthcoming for this battle: Cambuslang in the southern suburbs of Glasgow. This place already has Arthurian associations as the burial place of the great King's Northern British enemy, Caw. Perhaps he was killed in the battle. Other proposals include the Lothian coast near Bass Rock.

If Arthur killed Caw, it would certainly explain why Caw's son St Gildas did not mention Arthur in his book.

Not all of the Britons' campaigns were successful however - in the South, the Saxons were winning with regularity. The Anglo Saxon Chronicle records Aella and Cissa as having defeated the Britons at Andredes Cester and killed all the Britons who lived there.

The Britons in the South may have been losing battles, but Arthur still seemed unbeatable in the North:

The seventh battle was in the Caledonian Forest, that is, the Battle of Celidon Coit

The seventh battle site can clearly be identified as the Caledonian Forest in modern Scotland: Coed Celyddon. It may originally have stretched from the Solway to the Highlands.

Not all of Arthur's battles were on rivers and forests however - he also defended Roman garrisons, like his ancestors before him.

The eighth battle was in Guinnion fort, and in it Arthur carried the image of the holy Mary, the everlasting Virgin, on his shield, and the heathen were put to flight on that day, and there was great slaughter upon them, through the power of Jesus Christ and the power of the holy Virgin Mary, his mother.

This quote suffers from the same problems as that for the Battle of Badon in the Annales Cambriae: the Welsh words for shield and shoulder (Iscuit and Iscuid) possibly being confused. Geoffrey of Monmouth explains that Arthur bore armorial bearings of both cross and virgin. Guinnion is very similar to the Roman fort of Vinovium at Binchester, Durham. Again it is clear that the real King Arthur operated in the North of Britain.

The ninth battle was in the City of the Legion

The Urbe Legionis or "City of the Legions" causes problems because there were two cities so called: Caerleon and Chester, at either end of the Welsh border. It is also possible that York bore such a title and, indeed, York was the last city with a legion and so in the 5th century it would have been "the" City of the Legions.

The idea that many other Roman forts, like Carlisle or Exeter, once had similar names seems unlikely though; as does identification with the Battle of Dyrham. Chester was Caer Legion, while Caerleon was Caer Legion guar Uisc (that is "Caerleon-upon-Usk"), though the latter often lost its suffix. Chester appears to be the likeliest candidate. It was actually recorded in the Annales Cambriae as Urbs Legionis and was the site of a well-attested Battle of Chester in Dark Age times. Once again Arthur is strongly identified with a king in the North West.

We will discuss the final battles later, as they occured later in his career but for now we investigate Arthur's proverbial "knights" - the warriors who accompanied him in his battles and quests. Not just his closest friends and family - but his rank and file footsoldiers.

The Sixth Legion: The Original Knights of the Round Table

Legio VI Victrix was the legion based at York that was commanded by the Dux of Britain.

The sixth legion was founded by Octavian (the future emperor Augustus) in 41 BCE, as a copy of the Caesarian sixth legion, which was in the army of his rival Marc Antony. Perhaps veterans who had fought under Caesar joined Octavian's unit.

The legion was first deployed to Perugia, Italy and then, in 121, the emperor Hadrian visited Germania Inferior, where he ordered the construction of the Lower Rhine limes. The building activities were led by the governor, Platorius Nepos, a personal friend of Hadrian. Next year, the emperor visited Britain and took VI Victrix with him, together with Platorius, who now became governor of Britain. At the same time, VIIII Hispana came to Germania Inferior; it seems that the two legions traded places.

The soldiers of the sixth legion were now to build the British limes, which is better known as Hadrian's wall. (They built the section between Newcastle and Carlisle, and a bridge across the river Tyne near Newcastle.) The legion's new base was York, Around 130 miles from Hadrian's wall.

Later (between 139 and 142), units of VI Victrix helped constructing the Antonine wall, between Edinburgh and Glasgow.

In the years between 155 and 158, a widespread revolt occurred in northern Britain, requiring heavy fighting by the British legions. They suffered heavily, and reinforcements had to be brought in from the two Germanic provinces. At first, the Romans remained masters of the area between Hadrian's wall and the Antonine wall, but at the beginning of the reign of Marcus Aurelius, it was abandoned. Hadrian's wall once again marked the northern frontier of the Roman Empire.

One of the officers serving in the legion in ca.165-166 was Publius Helvius Pertinax, who was to be emperor for a brief period in 193. After his death, civil war broke out between several generals: Pescennius Niger in the east, Didius Julianus in Italy, Septimius Severus in the northeast, and Clodius Albinus in the west. The two last-mentioned pretenders concluded an alliance, which gave Severus the opportunity to eliminate Didius and Pescennius. In 196, he and Clodius started a second round of civil war. The British legions were ferried to the continent, but were defeated by Lucius Septimius Severus near Lyon.

When they returned, they found the province overrun by northern tribes and VI Victrix had to recapture and rebuild York. The soldiers also reconstructed parts of Hadrian's wall. At the same time, the unit was awarded the title Fidelis Constans ('loyal and steadfast'). Usually, this title was awarded after a unit had prevented a rebellion, but we know nothing about such an incident.

Lucius Artorius' position in the Legio VI Victrix, Prefect of the Legion (Praefectus Legionis), was equivalent to that of the Praefectus Castrorum.

Men who had achieved this title were normally 50–60 years old and had been in the army most of their lives, working their way up through the lower ranks and the centurionate until they reached Primus Pilus (the rank seems to have been held exclusively by primipilares).

They acted as third-in-command to the legionary commander, the Legatus Legionis, and senior tribune, and could assume command in their absence.

Their day-to-day duties included maintenance of the fortress and management of the food supplies, sanitation, munitions and equipment.

For most who had attained this rank, it would be their last before retirement, so, given his administrative position and (probably) advanced age, it is unlikely that Lucius Artorius actually fought in any battles while serving in Britain.

Artorius could have overseen vexillations of troops guarding Hadrian's Wall, but his inscriptions do not provide us with any precise information on where he might have served while in Britain. It has been suggested by the author Linda Malcor that he was stationed at Bremetennacum with a contingent of Sarmatians (originally sent to Britain in 175 AD) by emperor Marcus Aurelius, but there is no evidence to support such a conjecture.

Given his duties as Praefectus Legionis, it is reasonable to assume that he spent some - if not all - of his time in Britain at the VI Victrix's headquarters in York.

In 208, Septimius Severus came to Britain, in an attempt to conquer Scotland. VI Victrix moved to the north, where it shared a large fortress with II Augusta, at Carpow on the river Tay. During this war, it received the honorific title Britannica. From now on, the full name of the legion was VI Victrix Pia Fidelis Britannica. The conquests were abandoned at an unknown moment in the third century.

During this century, VI Victrix remained at York, and shared the fate of Britain. When this province was part of the Gallic Empire, it supported the Gallic emperors (260-274); when Britain became independent, it supported usurpers like Carausius and Allectus (286-297). After 297, the province was again incorporated in the Roman empire, and the soldiers served crown-prince (later emperor) Constantius I Chlorus. When he died in 306 in York, soldiers of the Sixth proclaimed his son emperor: Constantine the Great (306-337).

In the last third of the fourth century, Roman rule in Britain was increasingly threatened, and order had to be restored several times. VI Victrix must have suffered defeats. Yet, the legion still existed in the late fourth century. It may have been withdrawn to the continent in 402 by Stilicho, the supreme commander of the Roman forces in Western Europe during the reign of Honorius.

However it is evident the legion's command did remain in York. Coel fulfilled the role of Dux or Vortiporus. He most likely used the Roman name Agricola and lived to an old age.

Coel was succeeded by his grandsons Maximus (Masguid) and Ambrosius (Emrys) - Mar of Ebrauc and Pabo Post Prydain.

In their later years Mar of Ebrauc became known as Uthyr Pendragon (the chief of York) and his brother in much later stories as the Myrdinn Emrys (Merlin Ambrosius).

When Ambrosius retired he was succeeded as leader and Dux of the legion by his nephew Artorius (Arthwys ap Mar).

So far we have met the young Arthur, his parents and grandparents, aunts and uncles. We understand that his base was Camulod and his men were the Sixth Legion of York.

Now we have established the time and place of Arthur, we will look at some of his famous warriors. We begin with his most controversial, historically, but also his most important - Lancelot.

It may seem curious to begin with someone who was such a late edition to Arthurian tales - but we will find he was there from the start under different names.

Lancelot, Guinevere and Excalibur

SIR.LAVNCELOT.
AND.THE.WITCH.
HELLAWES.

Lancelot

We must understand that Lancelot was not introduced to Arthurian Romance until fairly late on. He was first mentioned by Chretien de Troyes but draws on earlier prototypes.

Lancelot, the Knight of the Cart is an Old French poem by Chrétien de Troyes. It is unknown exactly when the poem was composed, only that it would have been between 1175 and 1181 - just 40 years or so after Geoffrey of Monmouth.

The action centers on Lancelot's rescue of the queen after she has been abducted by Meleagant (Melwas, Maelgwyn Gwynedd). The abduction of Guinevere (Gwenhwyfar) is one of the oldest motifs in Arthurian legend, appearing also in Caradoc of

Llancarfan's Life of Gildas, and carved on the archivolt in Modena Cathedral.

Chrétien first mentions a character named "Lanceloz del Lac" in Erec and Enide, who he lists third among Arthur's knights after Gawain and Erec.

Roger Sherman Loomis (1887 – October 11, 1966) suggested that Lancelot is related to either the character Llenlleog the Irishman from Culhwch and Olwen or the Welsh hero Llwch Llawwynnauc.

Traditional scholars thought that they are the same figure, due to the fact that their names are similar and that they both wield a sword and fight for a cauldron in Preiddeu Annwn and Culhwch.

This is quite correct - the Lancelot character did draw upon this Welsh folklore but at the root of the folklore (intertwined with Irish mythology) was a real man - and his name was Llaenawc - and he was the brother of Arthur ap Mar.'

Much like Lancelot came from Llenlleog, the original folk hero simply came from Llaenawc. But we will see it is far more than a similar sounding name. All of Lancelot's main adventures take place between north Yorkshire and the Scottish lowlands - Arthur's kingdom.

And amazingly we find that Llaenauc was none other than the brother of Arthwys ap Mar. The significance of Lancelot is that he was originaly Arthur's brother!

Gwyr y Gogledd:

[G]uallauc map Laenauc map Masguic clop map Ceneu map Coyl hen

Gwallawg ap Llaenauc ap Masguid Gloff ap Ceneu ap Coel Hen

The earliest Arthurian legend is Culhwch and Olwen, where Arthur is helping his kinsman Culhwch on a quest. Culhwch is called Einion in some tales (Einion et Olwen).

Another relative of Arthur's is Mordred. Sometimes he is Arthur's brother, sometimes his nephew, sometimes his son.

In the later medieval stories, Lancelot is Arthur's closest friend and brother-in-arms. It is no surprise, then, to learn that Einion (Culhwch), Mordred and Llwch Lleminawc (Lancelot) all feature in the pedigrees of the north and are actually brothers of the real King Arthur.

We can easily see that Arthwys and his brother Llaenawc are Arthur and his first knight Lleminawc. If further proof were needed, Llaenawc's son was Gwallawg - the Galahad of legend and the famous son of Lancelot. Goodrich and Loomis made the same connection.

Goodrich wrote: "Loomis decided that there must have been a genetic connection between Lancelot and Irish nobility and specifically between him and King Lugh.

"Both, he pointed out, had been raised by queens and trained by 'sailors.'

"Both personages remained nameless during infancy - As soon as each prince arrived at court he occupied a special seat of honour - and was much admired for physical beauty..."

It has also been suggested that Arthur's brother's son, Eliwlod, the dialogue of Arthur and the Eagle is a prototype Lancelot:

Eagle of blameless aspect
And whose discourse is not evil,
Art thou Eliwlod my nephew?

Similarly Lot of Lothian and Lanval have linguistic similarities that make it possible they were originally the same character.

I would suggest that Llaenauc was the origin for all of them and via confusion with the Irish Lugh led to multiple characters - Lan-ce-Lot, Lan-Val and Eliw-Lod.

Lancelot and Excalibur

Arthur, crowned at 15 as a young soldier, would later lead his father's armies against the saxons, but first he was sent to fight the Irish. Maybe it was here that his sword began to become legendary itself, as the British Excalibur has its origins in the Irish sword Caladbolg.

Arthur and his brothers Llaenawc (Lancelot) and Einion (Culhwch) led the expedition, which is recorded in the legend of Culhwch and Olwen.

Culhwch and Olwen is a Welsh tale about a hero connected with Arthur and his warriors that survives in only two manuscripts: a complete version in the Red Book of Hergest, ca. 1400, and a fragmented version in the White Book of Rhydderch, ca. 1325. Certain linguistic evidence indicates it took its present form by the 11th century, making it perhaps the earliest Arthurian mythical tale and one of Wales' earliest extant prose texts. Lady Charlotte Guest included this tale among those she collected under the title The Mabinogion.

In Culhwch and Olwen, Arthur's retinue sail to Ireland (aboard his ship Prydwen) to obtain the cauldron of Diwrnach, who treats them to a feast but refuses to give up his prize.

Arthur's warrior Llenlleawc (based on the historical Llaenawc of Elmet) grabs Caladvwch (Excalibur) and kills Diwrnach's entire retinue.

Parallels between this episode and Preiddeu Annwfn may be found in a muddled passage from the latter, which contends that the "flashing sword of Lleawch" was raised to the cauldron, leaving it in the hands of "Lleminawc". Some scholars have opted to identify either or both Lleawch and Lleminawc with Culhwch's Llenlleawc, citing a confusion or evolution of names in the manuscript tradition. They are a combination of Llaenawc of Elmet and the Irish god Lugh.

But how do we know Arthwys had any connection with Ireland? Because it was in Ireland that Arthur (and the future 'Lancelot'...) met Arthur's future wife.

Guinevere

When this was announced to Queen Guinevere, she gave way to despair. She fled from York to the City of the Legions and there, in the church of Julius the Martyr, she took her vows among the nuns, promising to lead a chaste life. **Geoffrey of Monmouth**

The famous wife of King Arthur was Gwenhwyfar ferch Cywyrt (later Guinevere daughter of Leodegraunce) who famously became a nun when Arthur discovered her infidelity. The real King Arthur's wife also ended her days in the church. Gwenhwyfar comes from the Irish Findobair.

The Irish St Cywair was the wife of Arthwys ap Mar. The Irish Gwenhwyfar ferch Cywyrt was the wife of Arthur. We can see the similarities between Gwenhwyfar fetch Cywyrt and "Cywair." At the time, Cywair was an Irish princess, the king in Ireland was Leoghaire – while Gwenhwyfar's father was Leodegraunce. Once again we see where the linguistics have come from.

Geoffrey tells us that Arthur and Guinevere married in York - further evidence that it was Arthwys and Cywair the story was based upon.

Triad 56 of the Trioedd Ynys Prydein ("The Triads of the Island of Britain") lists the names and patronymics of the "Three Great Queens" of Arthur's court. To quote this triad in full: Three Great Queens of Arthur's Court: Gwennhwyfar daughter of Cywryt Gwent, And Gwenhwyfar daughter of Gwythyr son of Greidawl, And Gwenhwyfar daughter of (G)ogfran the Giant.

So how did Cywair become Gwenhwyfar? It may simply be that she was confused with one of Arthur's men named as Gwynn Hyvar. Both Gwenhwyfar and Gwynn Hyvar were at various times accused of causing civil war through gossip.

In later romances Arthur had no issue which is why he abdicated his kingdom to the son of Cador, whereas as the real Arthur ap Mar passed his throne to his son Keidyaw.

In earlier Welsh legends, Arthur is credited with many sons - and a few daughters. The most notable are:

- Amr (Amir. Anir, Amr Mor, Mor, Moroie Mor, Sir Amhar, possibly identical with Kyduan)
- Llacheu who is probably Sir Loholt
- Gwydre
- A nephew Cador

These correspond perfectly to the real Arthur's sons who were:

- Cinbelin (Amhar)
- Eleuther (Llacheu/Loholt)
- Greidol (Gwydre)
- Keidyaw (Cador)

Cinbelin is referred to also as Kyduan in Arthurian mythology, where it states he was the son of Arthur by his mistress Eleirch daughter of Iaen.

Eleirch verch Iaen mam Kyduan ap Arthur

Not only does Cywair have Guinevere's attributes, she also seems to be related to the Ceridwen of Welsh mythology.

Ceridwen is firmly associated with Bala Lake in North Wales. On the shores of this distinctly special lake, there is a sacred spring, noted for its magical powers. Nowadays, it is dedicated to St. Cywair—who is also known as Gwyr — who gives her name to the village of Llangower. Cywair/Gwyr is said to have been the mother of Llywarch Hen, another legendary bard — just like Ceridwen's son Taliesin.

Are Cywair and Ceridwen one and the same?

Did Llaenauc Command Arthur's Battles In the North?

In the previous chapter I suggested possible locations in the north for some of Arthur's battles, but now taking Llaenauc (Lancelot) into consideration as his right hand man, we can perhaps get a better picture.

Dubglas in Linuis

Arthur comes across the Pennines where he engages the Saxons at the Roman town of Coccium (now Wigan). They fight on the River Douglas, Lancs (Dubglas, Linuis). The battle may have been fought in the area now called Standish or near Blackrod.

Llaenauc (Lancelot) fights them at Britain's largest Lake (at the time) which is now called Martin Mere. He becomes known as Llaenauc of the Lake. Local legend states that Martin Mere was originally Myrdinn's Mere (Merlin's Lake) and that is why the Camelot theme park was built nearby.

18th century Mancunian historian, Rev John Whitaker points out that the Anglo-Saxon word for "lake" is "linuis" which today survives in its corrupted form – "Ince" which is part of Wigan. So was Llaenauc's stronghold Wigan?

Baines quotes extensively from Whitaker's History of Manchester (1795, vol. I): he equates 'Linnuis' with Martin Mere; repeats the local legend that, following Arthur's battle near Blackrod, the Douglas was crimsoned with blood as far as Wigan.

Arthurian traditions also abound in the local folklore of Martin Mere itself. It was supposedly into this lake that the nymph Vivian, mistress of Merlin, disappeared with the abducted infant Lancelot, and here in subterranean caverns beneath its waters, the child was educated. There is no denying that the Mere and its surrounding wetlands became a focus for many of his legends. This evocative, mysterious and extensive tract of water would inevitably attract Arthurian tradition.

A more speculative point would be - some of these myths contain shadows of even older beliefs. Those concerning Arthur's sword, and the nymph Vivian disappearing into the lake with the infant Lancelot, might conveniently mask earlier folk memories of gifts to a heathen fertility goddess or even human sacrifice. Some of the bog bodies of North Meols Moss and other places near the Mere suggest pagan practices.

Pagan customs clung on for a long time in Lancashire. In the nineteenth century Beltain fires were still lit on All Hallows' Eve (31 October).

Sir Lancelot's parents, King Ban of Benwick and his queen Elaine, escaped to Lancashire from France. Elaine went to help her husband who had fallen and put Lancelot down on the shore of the lake, from where he was abducted by a nymph, Vivian, who vanished into the waters of the lake with him.

When Lancelot went to Arthur's court he was knighted as 'Sir Lancelot of the Lake'. Martin Mere has been known as the 'Lost Lake of Sir Lancelot' following the myth.

Glein

Arthur and Llaenauc (Lancelot) defeats the Angles at the River Glein, near to Yeavering Bell, the largest iron age fort in Northumberland. It is close to Bamburgh. Llaenauc commanded from nearby Din Guayrdi. Bamburgh led to Lancelot's father being listed in the mythologies as Ban. His castle Din Guayrdi is known in legend as Dolorous Guard. Arthur sends Lllaenauc north of Hadrian's Wall to fight the Picts.

The Pictish Campaign

Bassas

Llaenauc defeats the Picts at Dunipace (Duin-na-bais hills of death). This is remembered in Lancelot's name "du lac" – of the Lake, since he was supposedly from "Lake Diana" (where the Lady of the Lake lived)

Tribruit

Traewruid along the River Forth was in the Bannockburn area. This led to the legend of Lancelot ruling Benwick (Bannock rather than the French Benoit).

Agned
Llaenauc defeated the Picts at Mount Agned (Edinburgh).

Asolat as Badon
Arthur and Llaenauc fights the Picts at Dunbarton. Asclud is remembered as the home of Lancelot – Asolat.

Celidon
Arthur defeats the Angles at the forest of Calaterium (Forest of Galtres north of Yorkshire). This is remembered by Geoffrey of Monmouth as Archgallo (he confused Arthwyrs with Arthegal) wandering in Calaterium forest; and later he says Arthur pursued the Saxons from Lichfield to Caledon.

Fortress of Guinnion
Arthur defeats the Angles at the Roman fortress of Vinovium (Binchester in Durham)

City of the Legion
Arthur defeats the Angles at the City of the Legion (Ebrauc - York).

Badon
Arthur defeats the Saxons at Caer Faddon as suggested in the Dream of Rhonabwy. Alternatively Buxton.

Wigan: Roman town of Coccium
The late 2nd-century Antonine Itinerary mentions a Roman settlement called Coccium 17 miles (27 km) from the Roman fort at Manchester (Mamucium) and 20 miles (32 km) from the fort at Ribchester (Bremetennacum).

Although the distances are slightly out, it has been assumed that Coccium is Roman Wigan.

Possible derivations of Coccium include from the Latin coccum, meaning "scarlet in colour, scarlet cloth", or from cocus, meaning "cook".

Roman finds from Wigan include coins, a Mithraic temple beneath the parish church, possible evidence for the remains of a Roman fort at Ship Yard and what is most likely a mansion - effectively a Roman hotel - with its own hypocaust and bath house.

Despite evidence of Roman activity in the area, there is no conclusive evidence of Wigan being the same site as Coccium, and it has been suggested that it could be located at Standish to the north of Wigan.

Heirs of Arthur: Cador, Amhar and Gwydre

Arthur and Cywair's sons, who would have been born in around 490-500AD were Keidyaw, Cinbelin, Greidal and Eleuther.

- Keidyaw became known as the Sir Cador of legend.
- Greidal and his son Gwythr are probably the origin of Arthur's mythical son Gwydre.
- The third son Eleuther was perhaps named after Arthur's father Uther and is the Llacheu of legend.
- Cinbelin, later the father of Cynwyd and grandfather of Cadrod, is the Amhar of legend.

Cador
We will meet Keidyaw/Cador in greater detail later on, but as we will see he was Arthur's chosen heir, much as Cador of legend was (in Geoffrey, Arthur left his throne to Cador's son Constantine).

Cinbelin-Amhar
In the early pedigrees, Cadrod's grandfather is Cinbelin, then the name Cinbelin is replaced by "Enir Fardd" - eventually Enir becomes Anir, then Amir and finally Amhar. Cinbelin may have taken his great uncle's title "father and pillar of Britain" since Pabo Post Prydain appears in some genealogies as Arthur's son not uncle – a case of confusing Ambrosius with Amhar.

Regardless, this is further evidence that Arthur ap Mar was the King Arthur of legend - both were the paternal great grandfather of Cadrod Calchfynedd.

The mythological King Arthur was the father of Amhar, father of Cynwyd, father of Cadrod

The historic Arthur ap Mar was the father of Cinbelin, father of Cynwyd, father of Cadrod.

In the Welsh Triads Pabo and Cinbelin (along with Gwallawc - see below - and Dunawd) are referred to as "pillars of Britain":

Three pillars of battle of the Island of Prydain. Dunawd son of Pabo pillar of Britain; and Gwallawc son of Lleenawc; and Cynfelyn Drwsgl.

In traditional Scots genealogies, Arthur's son Amhar is referred to as Mor, Morvie, Smervie or Moroie Mor – again showing his descent from King Mor – Uther Pendragon.

In the Scots traditions, he is born at Dunbarton and his son Ferither (Fer-Uther?) is the ancestor of the Macallan clan.

The fact that Arthur ap Mor and his son are also in Scots genealogies, suggests that the real King Arthur's rule did indeed extend past Hadrian's Wall.

Cadrod's descendant Yspwys is recorded as being a comrade of Uther and Ambrosius - although he lived too late to be so, he could have been connected to them in a genealogy.

Sir Galahad

As we have already seen from the legend of Culhwch, Llaenawc gained his reputation fighting alongside Arthur in Ireland and later became the Sir Lancelot of legend. Of course, the legendary Sir Lancelot's son was Galahad and the real Sir Lancelot's son was Gwallawc.

Just as Lancelot father of Galahad was the right-hand man of King Arthur, so too was Llaenawc father of Gwallawc the brother of Arthur ap Mar. Like Galahad, Gwallawc was a great knight and known as the Battle Horseman.

There are two surviving poems in praise of him, and it is one of these that identifies the Kingdom which was ruled by his line. In En env Gvledic nef gorchordyon, he is called "a judge over Elmet".

Ban of Benwick

In legend, Lancelot was the son of King Ban and he lived at 'Joyous Garde' - unsurprisingly we find the real Joyous Garde in the North of Britain.

In the Arthurian legends, the evil Sir Brian of the Isles lived at Dolorous Guard. It was a dangerous enchanted place, where knights passing by would find themselves obliged to fight two sets of ten knights at the two gates. They were never successful and were locked up in the nearby Dolorous Prison, while memorial gravestones marked their demise. Eventually, with the help of several magical shields, Sir Lancelot defeated the mystical knights and released all the prisoners. Sir Brian fled to Pendragon Castle and Lancelot took on Dolorous Guard as his new home. However, in order to free the castle residents completely from their enchantment, Lancelot had to stay there for forty consecutive nights. The menacing gravestones magically disappeared and Lancelot decided to rename the place as Joyous Guard.

Once again, both Lancelot and Galahad are firmly in the north, as are of course their historic counterparts Llaenawc and Gwallawc.

The castle's story mostly appears in the Vulgate Cycle (1215), where it is said to be in Northumberland. Sir Thomas Malory (1470) more specifically states that "some men say it was Alnwick, and some men say it was Bamborough".

The first historical mention of Bamburgh Castle occurs in Nennius' Historia Brittonum (AD 829) where it is stated that "Aethelfrith the Artful reigned twelve years in Bernicia and another twelve in Deira. He reigned twenty-four years in the two kingdoms, and gave Din Guayrdi to his wife, whose name was Bebba, and it was named Babbanburth from his wife's name"

"Ida son of Eobba held the countries in the north of Britain, that is, north of the Humber Sea, and reigned twelve years, and joined Din Guayrdi to Bernicia".

It is clear that Lancelot's legendary castle was not invented by medieval writers. From these references, it is evident that Bamburgh's original name was Din Guayrdi, a Celtic-British place- name meaning "Fort of the Guayrdi". The Guayrdi are presumed to have been a sub-tribe of the Brigantes, a major pre-Roman tribal coalition which covered most of the North of England.

The stronghold was only taken over by the Northern Anglo-Saxons during the mid-6th century reign of King Ida of Bernicia and its name changed by his grandson, King Aethelfrith.

Aethelfrith's wife, Bebba, was herself a Celt and it seems that this is why she became particularly associated with the old British fortress.

The British origins of Bamburgh are further confirmed by the 12th century chronicler, Geoffrey Gaimar, who, drawing upon older sources, wrote that King Ida "restored Bamborough. It was much decayed and ruined since Ebrauc built it long ago."

And here we have proof that Ebrauc-Iubher-Uther was also the name of a person. Joyous Garde was in fact built by the great Uther. It is spelled out for us that Ebrauc was an eponymous man of York - and that was of course King Mar (Uther). And of course he was the father of Llaenauc. It is clear that Bamburgh alias Din-Guayrdi was an important Celtic stronghold in the British Kingdom of Bryneich, long before the Saxons took over and renamed the country Bernicia. Its natural defences encouraged the Romano-British to continue occupying the old Roman beacon there in the troubled times after the departure of the Imperial administration.

The Bryneich Kings were one of several branches of these descendants of old King Coel, the last Roman Dux Brittanniarum. In fact, the Bryneich monarch who was contemporary with King Arthur and Sir Lancelot was King Bran Hen (the Old), a man who can only have been the origin of Lancelot's father Ban of Benwick.

The identification of Arthur with Arthur ap Mar becomes more and more clear as we add more pieces to the jigsaw - we are now starting to see the whole family tree dropping into place and seeing that every Arthurian character was part of the same dynasty. So far we have introduced the real Arthur, Guinevere, Uther, Igraine, Constans, Merlin Emrys, Lancelot, Galahad, Ban, Cador, Amhar, Gwydre, Morgan, Anna, Niniane, Culhwch and of course Camelot, Joyous Garde and Excalibur.

King Mark

In Arthurian legends, Mark of Cornwall was a king of Dumnonia or Kernow in the early 6th century. He is most famous for his appearance in Arthurian legend as the uncle of Tristan and husband of Iseult, who engage in a secret affair behind his back.

Mark sent Tristan as his proxy to fetch his young bride, the Princess Iseult from Ireland. Tristan and Iseult fall in love, and, with the help of a magic potion, proceed to have one of the stormiest love affairs in medieval literature.

Mark suspects of the affair and eventually, his suspicions are confirmed. In some versions, he sends for Tristan to be hanged, and Iseult sent to a leper colony. Tristan escapes the hanging and rescues Mark's bride from her confinement, later to be discovered by Mark. Mark eventually forgives them, with Isolde returning to Mark and Tristan leaving the country.

In the Prose Tristan, Mark's character deteriorates from a sympathetic cuckold to a downright villain. He rapes his niece and then murders her when she produces his son, Meraugis, and he murders his brother Baldwin as well. In earlier versions of the story, Tristan dies in Brittany, far away from Mark, but in the Prose Tristan, Mark stabs Tristan while he plays the harp under a tree for Iseult. Though this version of Mark's character was popular in other medieval works, including the Romance of Palamedes and Sir Thomas Malory's Le Morte d'Arthur, modern versions of the Tristan and Iseult legend tend to take their inspiration from the older poetic material, and Mark becomes a sympathetic character once again. In these legends Mark is usually seen as ruling Cornwall from Tintagel Castle.

In Wrmonoc of Landévennec's Life of St. Pol de Leon, he refers to a "King Marc whose other name is Quonomorus". This gives us a clue as to who the real Marc or Quonomorus were - they were in fact two separate people and they were father and son.

Meirchion the Lean, presumably a very slim man, was the son of Gurgust, son of Ceneu. He succeeded his father as King of a united Rheged, though Ceneu passed Elmet and Ebrauc to his son Mar and the Pennines to Pabo.

Meirchion had a son called Cynfarch ap Meirchionn (Cunomorus son of Marcus) who would seem to be the King Cunomorus - Mark of legend.

Cynfarch's unflattering epithet Oer means 'the Dismal'. He was the son of Meirchion Gul, the King of Greater Rheged and, upon his father's death, inherited the Northern portion of his Kingdom.
The 'Mote of Mark,' near Palnackie (Kirkcudbright in Scotland) has revealed much evidence of Dark Age occupation.
Some associate it with the legendary King Mark of Cornwall, but the home of King Cyn-Mark of North Rheged is much more likely. Also, near Stranraer is Dunragit, a fortified hillfort location named as the 'Fort of Rheged'. Cynfarch was eventually succeeded by his son, Urien.

Gorlois, Urien and Mark in the mythological tree:

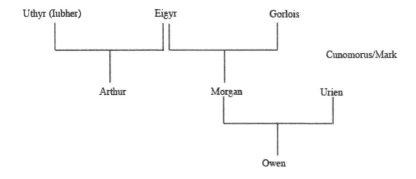

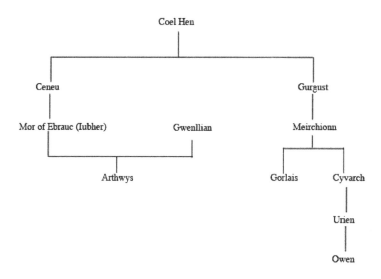

Gorlais, Urien and Meirchionn in the historic tree

Sir Tristan

The historical Tristan was a Pictish prince. Since he and the real King Mark were contemporaries in what is now Scotland, there could be a shred of truth to the stories of Tristan and Isolde.

King lists of Picts are very difficult to reconcile, since the Picts had a matriarchal society and inheritance was passed through the female line.

Mists of Avalon: Merlin and Morgan

Ambrosius Aurelianus (Pabo Post Prydain) was Arthur's advisor.
As the boy Emrys he is the basis for the mythical Merlin Emrys.

Geoffrey of Monmouth's account of Merlin Ambrosius' early
life in the Historia Regum Britanniae is based on the story of
Ambrosius in the Historia Brittonum.

He adds his own embellishments to the tale, which he sets in
Carmarthen (Caer Myrdinn). While Nennius' Ambrosius
eventually reveals himself to be the son of a Roman consul,

Geoffrey's Merlin is begotten on a king's daughter by an incubus. The story of Vortigern's tower is essentially the same; the underground dragons, one white and one red, represent the Saxons and the British, and their final battle is a portent of things to come.

At this point, Geoffrey inserts a long section of Merlin's prophecies, taken from his earlier Prophetiae Merlini. He tells only two further tales of the character; in the first, Merlin creates Stonehenge as a burial place for Aurelius Ambrosius. In the second, Merlin's magic enables Uther Pendragon to enter into Tintagel in disguise and father his son Arthur on his enemy's wife, Igraine. These episodes appear in many later adaptations of Geoffrey's account.

As the Arthurian mythos was retold and embellished, Merlin's prophetic aspects were sometimes de-emphasized in favour of portraying Merlin as a wizard and elder advisor to Arthur.

In the Lancelot-Grail and later accounts, Merlin's eventual downfall came from his lusting after a woman named Nimue, one of the maidens serving the Lady of the Lake, who coaxed his magical secrets from him before turning her new powers against her master and trapping him in an enchanted prison (variously described as a cave, a large rock, an invisible tower, etc.) This is unfortunate for Arthur, who has lost his greatest counsellor.

The name "Myrddin" may have arisen from the Roman-period Celtic name for a place in Wales, Moridunon, meaning "sea fort". It is interesting that the real Merlin's brother was also called Mor.

Perhaps in their early adventures together Masguid (Uther) gained the nickame Mor (sea) and his brother Ambrosius (Pabo) gained the nickname Moridunon (sea fort). We should note that one of Mor's sons was called Morydd and the name is also seen in the mythical Morrigan, which may have contributed to the legend of Morgan Le Fay.

Morgan le Fay, alternatively known as Morgane, Morgain, Morgana and other variants, is a powerful sorceress and antagonist of King Arthur and Guinevere in the Arthurian legend.

The early works featuring Morgan do not elaborate her character beyond her role as a fay or magician. She became much more prominent in the later cyclical prose works such as the Lancelot-Grail and the Post-Vulgate Cycle, in which she is said to be the daughter of Arthur's mother, the Lady Igraine, and her first husband, Gorlois, Duke of Cornwall; Arthur is her half brother by Igraine and Uther Pendragon and elsewhere, she is married, unhappily, to King Urien of Gore and Ywain is her son.

Morgan's role is greatly expanded in the 13th century Lancelot- Grail (Vulgate Cycle) and the subsequent works inspired by it. Morgan continues her magical studies under Merlin. In some legends she seduces Merlin, and in others this role is taken by Nimue. Not surprisingly there seems to be some basis in fact of Merlin Emrys' relationship with the real Morgan Le Fay.

St Madrun was the wife of Emyr Guent (maybe Ambrosius/Emrys of Gwent) and they were the parents of Honorious of Gwent (Ynyr Guent).

Another son of Madrun is St Ceidyaw. I wonder if Madrun having a son called Ceidyaw and Arthur having a son called Keidyaw led some to believe that Arthur had an incestuous relationship with Morgan?

Regardless, we see that both Myrddin Emrys (Pabo) and Morgan (Madrun) were closely related to Arthwys and very probably knew each other well.

Gawain

Gawain, also called Gwalchmei, Gawan, Gauvain, Walewein, etc.) is usually depicted as King Arthur's nephew and a Knight of the Round Table who appears very early in the Arthurian legend's development. He is one of a select number of Round Table members to be referred to as the greatest knight, most notably in Sir Gawain and the Green Knight. He is almost always portrayed as the son of Arthur's sister Morgause (or Anna) and King Lot of Orkney and Lothian, and his brothers are Agravain, Gaheris, Gareth, and Mordred.

Gawain is commonly considered identical with the Welsh hero known as Gwalchmei (or Gwalchmai) ap Gwyar, who appears in the Welsh Triads and in Culhwch and Olwen, an Arthurian romance associated with the Mabinogion. His appearance in Culhwch, which probably dates to the 11th century, makes him one of the earliest characters associated with Arthur.

Culhwch says of Gawain (Gwalchmai):
Arthur called on Gwalchmei, son of Gwyr, because he never came home without the quest he had gone to seek. He was the best of walkers, and the best of riders. He was Arthur's nephew, his sister's son, and his first cousin.

If Gawain was the son of Lot of Lothian, we would expect to find the historical Gawain in Scotland - and that is where we find him in the form of Gabran of Dalriada.

Gabrán mac Domangairt was king of Dál Riata in the middle of the 6th century. The historical evidence for Gabrán is the notice of his death in the Irish annals.

Kings of Alba and of Scotland traced their descent through Gabrán to his grandfather Fergus Mór, who was seen as the ultimate founder of the royal house as late as the 16th and 17th centuries.

Gabran's wife Lluan was the daughter of Gwenllian's brother Brychan II making Lluan the first cousin of King Arthur.

The name Gabran was preserved in the legend of Sir Gawain as his sword was supposed to have been given to him by "Gaban". Once again we see another key Arthurian character in the north.

The Breaking of Camelot

XCIII Annus. Gueith Camlann, in qua Arthur et Medraut corruere; et mortalitas in Brittania et in Hibernia fuit.

Year 93 (539 AD) The strife of Camlann, in which Arthur and Medraut fell, and there was death in Britain and in Ireland.

The Annales Cambriae C900AD

Arthur's victories against the Saxons did not hold his kingdom of Camelot together for long. The Arthurian stories tell us of many challenges he faced from his own people. The first was from Sir Caradoc.

In 495AD the Anglos Saxon Chronicle records Cerdic as having arrived in Britain. But Cerdic is not a Saxon name - it is a British name seen in variants like Caradoc and Carados.

Cerdic would have been the mortal enemy of Arthur. They lived at exactly the same time. Arthur was leading the Britons to victory in the North as Cerdic was leading the Saxons in the South. And the pedigrees list Cerdic as a brother of Arthwys.

If Cerdic were Arthur's enemy, in Arthurian legends Cerdic seems to be represented by Sir Caradoc of the Dolorous Tower. Often called "the Huge," Sir Caradoc was a vast man, thought of by some as a giant. He was the son of Mitrides (or Aupatris) and the brother of Sir Turquine. The two appeared together at the Castle Dangerous Tournament. Caradoc had a son named, Karakadin. He had been a Knight at the Court of Uther Pendragon, but did not get on with King Arthur.

Caradoc was perhaps the best known of the evil lords of the realm who liked nothing better than to capture Knights of the Round Table and throw them into the most wretched of prisons. In this case at the, aptly named, Dolorous Tower. The numbers of prisoners grew so large - including Sir Yvain and Sir Gawain - that King Arthur was forced to declare war on Caradoc. The Dolorous Army held off the King's forces at the Wicked Pass, but Sir Lancelot broke through to engage their leader in single combat. The Lady Florée gave Lancelot a magic sword and Caradoc was slain.

In 501 Saxons under Port, Bieda and Maegla came to Britain and immediately won a battle, and in 508 Cerdic's troops defeated the Briton Natanleod.

However - was Cerdic coming to Britain for the first time or was he, like Arthur a Romanised Briton who had been campaigning in Ireland or France? In around 510 Arthur won more keys battles and the British hope was reignited - it is recorded by Nennius.

The tenth battle was on the bank of the river called Tribruit Tribruit, more properly Tryfrwyd.

The battle is mentioned in an eleventh century Welsh poem from the Black Book of Carmarthen, Pa Gur (covered later in the book). Some people identify its location as the River Frew at Stirling; others, the River Ribble in Lancashire; or the Eden at Carlisle.

The eleventh battle was on the hill called Agned

Geoffrey of Monmouth identifies Monte Agned as Edinburgh, and there appears to be little evidence to contradict him. The rock of Edinburgh Castle was certainly occupied at this time. It was a strategic point of some importance at the centre of the Kingdom of Gododdin. Perhaps the battle was connected with King Lot of Gododdin being one of the eleven kings who rebelled against Arthur at the beginning of his reign. Edinburgh, alias Din-Eityn specifically relates to the settlement on top of the rock of course.

In 514 more of Cerdic's troops landed and defeated the Britons. But Arthur would strike back in his greatest victory: Badon.

The Battle of Badon

The twelfth battle was on Badon Hill and in it nine hundred and sixty men fell in one day, from a single charge of Arthur's, and no-one lay them low save he alone.

It was in 516 or 518 (the Annales Cambrae can be ambiguous), at the Battle of Mount Badon, where tradition says the Saxon advance into Britain was finally halted. It was Arthur's greatest victory and, not surprisingly, there are many claimants for its location. Forts are preferred, since Gildas, in his De Excidio Britanniae, more properly called the battle a "siege". Possibilities include Bowden Hill, Lothian; and Dumbarton Rock, Strathclyde and thirdly, Buxton which we will come to later. I disregard Bath as a possibility since it is too flat and too far south.

Gildas writes "ad annum obsessionis Badonici montis ... quique quadragesimus quartus ut novi orditur annus mense iam uno emenso qui et meae nativitatis est", which has been translated in more than one way.

It may mean "at/to the year of the siege of Mount Badon ... which happened 44 years and one month since, a fact I know as it is my birth".

This is often said to mean Gildas was born the year of Badon but possibly - just possibly - it could be he was born at Badon. And Gildas was born in Dumbarton.

Arthur's opponent at Badon, according to the Dream of Rhonabwy, was Osla Big Knife. This is the historic Esa, Jute invader of Northumbria who was succeeded after Badon by his son Eoppa. Eoppa was succeeded by his son Ida.

If Octa was really a Northumbrian it would stand to reason that Badon was fought by Arthwys of Ebrauc.

Another interesting theory is that Badon is where the Dream of Rhonabwy identify it – as Caer Faddon. This isn't too far from where a Northern Arthur could have fought at Lichfield, as described by Geoffrey of Monmouth.

Geoffrey has Arthur pursuing the Saxons from Lichfield (Staffordshire) to the Forest of Caledon. It is only two days' ride from Lichfield to Wroxeter (Viriconium) and on to Welshpool, where The Dream of Rhonabwy places Badon at Caer Faddon. The retreat by the Saxons to"Thanet" could be to the River Tanat, just west of Breidden.

In his Arthurian sourcebook The Mammoth Book of King Arthur, Mike Ashley weighs up 20 historic leaders who could have been the real King Arthur. Of Arthwys of the Pennines (Arthur ap Mar) he states:

"The number of sites in the north that could relate to Nennius's battle list is sufficiently tempting to suggest that there was an Arthur of the North, probably resident in Elmet, whose exploits against the Angles were long remembered.

"Arthwys us the best situated to fight a campaign along the eastern frontier which, because of its association with Gildas' partition, is the one most likely to be connected with Badon.

"Just possibly, despite the other great and powerful at Badon, it was the northern prince who saved the day and entered legend. It may even be just as Geoffrey described it, with Arthwys pursuing the Saxons from Lichfield to a last ditch battle."

Ashley suggests the following scenario:

"Arthwys of the Pennines was fighting a sustained campaign against the Saxons along the eastern frontier. His forces were stretched to the south, which allowed a retaliation by Aelle...

"Aelle's forces... pushed further west and were met by a coalition of kings... along the western frontier, resulting in a siege...

"Arthwys was able to bring is forces into play and wiped out the Saxon force. Aelle, Bretwalda of the Saxons was killed, and thereafter the Saxons lacked a figurehead.

"The coalition of kings was now able to dictate a boundary which the Saxons could not cross, a boundary which Arthwys may have continued to patrol from his base at Lichfield. Arthwys maintained a peace in Britain until his death... in the 530s... This is likely to have been near the [northern] frontier, perhaps at Camboglanna, which is why it would also be remembered in Y Gododdin.

"I suspect he found this in his Northern Chronicle, which he tried to blend with the elements in Nennius and Gildas. If it were ever possible to prove that either Arthwys ap Mar or Elifer fought at Lichfield and Caer Faddon, then we would have found Geoffrey's Arthur."

Indeed we have found Geoffrey's Arthur – we have found King Arthur!

The principle of Ockham's Razor basically states that the simplest explanation is most likely the correct one. There have been many theories as to whom the real King Arthur was, and many are so convoluted as to be ridiculous.

Lawrence Gardner claims Arthur was a combination of Artur of Dalriada (who he says was married to someone called Gwenhwyfar - he wasn't) and Arthur of Dyfed (who he pushes back a hundred years and says was married to Guanhumara - he wasn't).

Blackett and Wilson state that Arthur was a mixture of Andragasius, apparently a son of Magnus Maximus and Athrwys of Gwent, who they push back nearly 200 years.

Other accounts suggest Arthur was a title used by Riothamus, Ambrosius or Cadell.

Of course the most likely explanation is that King Arthur was really, well, a king called Arthur or Arthwys - one who lived in the right time and place.

In order to get their theories to fit, some authors have claimed the Annales Cambrae got dates wrong, Nennius was really talking about Uriens, Arthur was later shoe-horned into the Welsh triads and many more conspiracies.

The simplest solution is that we should look to the earliest mentions of Arthur to determine what we are looking for:

Therefore we are looking for someone born in about 470, fighting from about 485 to 516 (from age 15 to age 45) where he was proclaimed chief of the kings, and then as an old man in about 540 fighting at Camlann.

There is only one candidate: Arthwys of the Pennines. He was a king, he was called Arthur and he lived at the same time as the King Arthur of legend.

The Other Badon - Buxton

Another theory for the location of Badon is Buxton in the High Peak area of Derbyshire. Right in Arthwys' Brigantes heartland, it was previously called Aquae Arnemetiae because of its Roman baths, and was referred to as Bathamgate.

If Bath can be Badon, so then can Buxton and unlike Bath, Buxton is both hilly and far enough north.

The Small Towns of Roman Britain records: "The town lies at the crossing of two main roads; that from Little Chester to Mancgester and that from Brough-on-Nie across the moors to Buxton and on then towards the Stone-on-Trent district; the first section is called Bathamgate.

"Fort or no, there were reasons enough for Buxton to develop as a small town in the Roman period. The existence of both hot and cold chalybeate springs and of an important religious sanctuary."

Buxton Civic Association records: "At Buxton's warm springs, the Celtic goddess of the grove was worshipped. 2000 years ago the Romans developed the first spa, Aquae Arnemetiae."

Whittaker's 'History of Manchester' published in 1773 records: "The Roman bagnio at this place was plainly discernable by the ruins, within the present century. The dimensions were then traceable by the eye, and the wall of it was brick still rising about a yard in height upon three sides and covered with a red coat of Roman cement as hard as brick and resembling tiles. The basin was floored with stones and supplied, not by any of the springs which feed the present bath immediately above, but by that finer source of water which is now called St. Anne's Well and was then enclosed within it; and this contained the very curious and only remains of the Roman baths in the district so late as the year 1709, when Sir Thomas Delves, with a Gothic generosity of spirit, destroyed the whole in order to cover the spring with the stone alcove that is over it at present. But about 50 yards to North East of this, driving a level from the present bath to the river, in 1697 was found an appendage probably to the Roman bagnio; a basin about four yards square but made with sheets of lead which were spread upon large beams of timber and broken ledges all along the borders. This additional bath was replenished from another spring which is about 14 yards from the south side of it called Bingham Well."

Professor Ian Richmond said of Buxton in his standard work 'Roman Britain': "The site was in military occupation on the fringe of the military area. The social pleasures of such spas counted for at least as much as their curative qualities, and they were pleasant resorts for soldiers or officials on leave or for civilians on holiday."

August Hunt in his article Glein to Camlan writes:

"Neil Bettridge, Archivist, Derbyshire County Council's Record Office, cites (via personal correspondence) Kenneth Cameron's "The Place-Names of Derbyshire", volume I, Cambridge University Press, 1959, regarding Bathamgate:

"On page 21, in the Roads and Ways section, Cameron records that Bathamgate is very probably 'the Bathum road', the first element Bathum being the dative plural baðum of bæd, 'bath or bathing place' in Old English. He cites his sources, with dates, as follows: Bathinegate (for Bathmegate), 1400, from W. Dugdale's Monasticon Anghcanum, 6 vols, London 1817-1830. Bathom gate, 1538, from Ancient Deeds in the Public Record Office. Batham Gate, 1599, from records of the Duchy of Lancaster Special Commissions in the Public Record Office."

Unlike the southern candidates for "Badon Hill" - Buxton is actually on top of a hill and surrounded by many.

Hunt writes: "If the grove of the goddess Nemetia continued as an important shrine well into Arthur's time (and the presence of St. Anne's Well at the site of the town's ancient baths shows that the efficacy of the sacred waters was appreciated well into Christian times), there is the possibility the Saxons targeted Buxton for exactly this reason. Taking the Britons' shrine would have struck them a demoralizing blow. If the goddess or saint or goddess-become-saint is herself not safe from the depredations of the barbarians, who is? "A threat to such a shrine may well have galvanized British resistance. Arthur himself may have been called upon to lead the British in the defense of Nemetia's waters and her temple-grove."

What could be more promising for King Arthur fighting at Badon than Arthwys ap Mar fighting at Batham and defending a "lady of the lake?"

View of Buxton 100 years ago

Cerdic or Caradoc

Arthur may have defeated the Saxons in 12 successive battles and checked the invasions but he still had to contend with his ambitious brother Cerdic.

It would appear that Cerdic was initially loyal to Arthur, where he is represented by Caradoc Vreichvras.

Since the crucial element is who - Geoffrey Caradog Strong-Arm was an early ancestor of the Kings of Gwent and, as such, should be identified with Caradog ap Ynyr, mentioned in the Life of St. Tathyw. Welsh legend calls his father Llyr Marini (of the Sea), while Breton legend indicates a Caradog the Elder. The former may have been a title in honour of the Celtic Sea-God, Llyr. But more than likely, Llyr Marini indicates his parentage from Uther, whose other name was Mor (sea).

His disputed parentage is, in fact, the basis of an Arthurian literary tale. Caradog's mother was said to have been an unfaithful wife, for the Caradog was her offspring by a lowly druid named Eliafres. While holding court at Caer-Ceri (Cirencester), Caradog confronted this man concerning the matter. Eliafres refused to answer his questions and caused a serpent to entwine itself around the young man's arm. It took the combined strength of both his wife, Tegau, and his friend, Cado, to remove the creature. The serpent, however, grasped Tegau's breast instead and she was forced to cut it off. Caradog's arm had shrivelled away and the, once strong, King Caradog thus became known as "Briefbras" or Short-Arm! Queen Tegau took to wearing an artificial gold breast, hence her epithet of "Eurfron" or Golden Breast. Welsh tradition tells of Tegau's story without mentioning Caradog's parental confusion.

The Welsh Triads, not surprisingly, portray Caradog deputising for the High-King Arthur at court in the City of the Legions.

Perhaps after Badon, when Arthur basked in the glory of repelling the Saxon invasions, Cerdic saw an opening to gain glory for himself. He proclaimed himself King in what is now Wessex and gathered armies from Saxon mercenaries.

Sir Mordred

Cerdic was not Arthur's only brother to apparently betray him. His brother Morydd, the Mordred of mythology, also rallied in civil war against Arthur. It may be that Mordred's name is derived from another Hadrian's Wall post where he was Moderatus.

Mordred or Modred (Welsh: Medraut, Medrod, etc.) is a character in the Arthurian legend, known as a notorious traitor who fought King Arthur at the Battle of Camlann, where he was killed and Arthur fatally wounded. Tradition varies on his relationship to Arthur, but he is best known today as Arthur's illegitimate son by his half-sister Morgause.

The illegitimacy angle was introduced in the Lancelot-Grail (Vulgate) Cycle, and has been taken up in most subsequent versions. In those versions, the incest is usually accidental; the participants are ignorant of their kinship. In one version Morgause mistakes Arthur for her husband visiting her in the night. In another Arthur rapes his sister, overtaken by lust for her. In any case, the discovery of the incest is usually disastrous.

A number of Welsh sources also refer to Medraut, usually in relation to Camlann. One triad, based on Geoffrey's Historia, provides an account of his betrayal of Arthur in another, he is described as the author of one of the "Three Unrestrained Ravagings of the Isle of Britain" – he came to Arthur's court at Kelliwic in Cornwall, devoured all of the food and drink, and even dragged Gwenhwyfar (Guinevere/Cywair) from her throne and beat her.

Medraut is never considered Arthur's son in Welsh texts, only his nephew or brother, though The Dream of Rhonabwy mentions that the king had been his foster father. However, Mordred's later characterisation as the king's villainous son was confused by the figure of Amr, a son of Arthur's known from only two references.

Virtually everywhere Mordred appears, his name is synonymous with treachery. A few works of the Middle Ages and today, however, portray Mordred as less a traitor and more a conflicted opportunist, or even a victim of fate. Mordred remains a major villain in many modern takes on the legend, including John Boorman's film Excalibur.

A picture now begins to develop. Arthur, the conquering hero with Cerdic (Caradoc) and Morydd (Mordred) as the jealous brothers.

Sir Amhar

Variously called Anir, Amir or Amr, the proper Welsh form is Amhar. He was a little known son of King Arthur and, presumably, Queen Guinevere. Amhar served as the King's squire and guarded his bedchamber. Nennius tells us that he was killed by his own father under unknown circumstances and buried within a cairn called Llygad Amr in Ergyng. The place is now called Gamber Head (Herefordshire). His grave is one of the "Marvels of Britain":

There is another wonder in the region, which is called Ercing. A tomb is located there next to a spring which is called Licat Amr; and the name of the man who is buried in the tomb was called thus: Amr. He was the son of Arthur the soldier, and Arthur himself killed and buried him in that very place. And men come to measure the grave and find it sometimes six feet in length, sometimes nine, sometimes twelve, sometimes fifteen. At whatever length you might measure it at one time, a second time you will not find it to have the same length - and I myself have put this to the test.

There is only one other surviving mention of this individual. A page called Amhar, son of Arthur, likely identical with the Historia's Amr, guards the king's bedchamber in the Welsh Romance Gereint and Enid, associated with the Mabinogion. That his stature is insufficient for Amhar to appear more than once (or even first in the list of Arthur's pages) points to illegitimacy.

Amr may have been a nickname as an abbreviated form of Ambrosius, Amlawdd or Amlach - names of his grandparents and uncles. Or perhaps A-Mor in tribute to his grandfather.

Amr's real name was Cinbelin (Kynvelin), a variation on the old Celtic name Cunobelinus or Cymbeline. He established himself in the territory of Gododdin among the northern Votadini with his base near Dunbar. One ancient chronicle suggests Cinbelin was a Brigantian warleader who took an army north and imposed himself on the Votadini. Amr and Cinbelin are interchangeable as grandfather of Cadrod in old pedigrees.

Amhar (Kynvelin) crops up in Welsh Arthurian tales and he is known as Kyduan, the son of Arthur and his mistress Eleirch.

Culhwch and Bonedd yr Arwyr indicate that Arthur had a relationship with Eleirch daughter of Iaen, which produced a son named Kyduan.

The mythological Arthur had a bastard son called Kyduan, the historic Arthwys had a son called Kynvelin.

Arthur was the son of Iubher and father of Kyduan.
Arthwys was the son of Iubher and father of Kynvelin.

Arthur was succeeded by Cador's son.
Arthwys was succeeded by Keidyaw.

Arthur had a brother, nephew or son called Modred.
Arthwys had a brother called Morydd.

Arthur's earliest companions were Llaenaog and Einion (Culhwch)
Arthwys' brothers were Llaenauc and Einion.

The Round Table

The real Round Table amazingly enough still bears the name of Arthur and Guinevere!

After Badon, Arthur left the Northern Roman HQ and relocated from Camulod to North Wales where he held court in Dyfed (more on this later). The British centre shifted from York to Wales as the Saxons advanced. We can see this by the location of Pabo's burial.

Meini Gwyr is named after Gwyr (and alternative spelling of Cywair). Its alternative name is Buarth Arthur and it is in Caermarthen, which, legend has it, was the home of Merlin Emrys – with the name Caer Myrddin.

Therefore Meini Gwyr references Arthwys (Buarth Arthur), Cywair (Gwyr) and Pabo (Myrddin).

It is an ancient henge of significance to the pagan Britons. The text on the information sign at the site reads as follows:

Meini Gwyr, also known as Buarth Arthur, is an embanked stone circle probably dating to the transition between the late Neolithic and early Bronze Age periods (c.2000BC). The site is likely to have been used for religious rituals.

The stone circle was the proverbial round table. According to a late 17thC account by Edward Lhuyd, there were then fifteen stones in the circle ranging in height from three to six feet, but a further seven or eight were thought to have been 'carried off'. Apparently, there was also an entrance lined by smaller slabs.

The site was partially excavated in 1938 by Professor W.F. Grimes. Unfortunately most of the records were destroyed in a bombing raid on Southampton in 1940.

The plan is based partly on ground and air photographs of the excavation. Grimes established that the circle, some 60 feet in diameter, originally consisted of 17 stones which, like the two surviving ones, were set at an angle into the inner slope of the bank about 3 feet hight and 120 feet in the external diameter, with no trace of a ditch.

The excavations confirmed that the entrance through the earth-work was formerly flanked by upright stones, set in a trench. Some fragments of early Bronze Age pottery came from a hearth set in a deep depression on the southeast bank.

Meini Gwyr stands at the centre of West Wales' most important complex of Neolithic and Bronze Age ritual and funerary monuments, lying on a ridge-way linking the western end of the Preselis to the eastern Cleddau river and Milford Haven.

This was a route by which the bluestones for Stonehenge may have been transported. Included in the complex are several Bronze Age burial mounds and cairns or various forms, and a 'henge' monument (akin to early elements at Stonehenge). Also, there is the site of 'Yr Allor' ('The Altar') comprising two, formerly three standing stones some 200 yards west of Meini Gwyr and apparently known by the 17thC. These stones may be the remains of a chambered tomb.

The name Cywair, being seen as Guinevere, is found at Cywair's Well or Gwyr's Well, from where Llangower is named. St Cywair's church remains in Llangower.

Legend also says that there was another well in this area, but that it now lies under the waters of Lake Bala (Llyn Tegid).

Apparently the well keeper forgot to put the cover over the well. This caused the spirit who lived in the well to become angry and the water gushed out forming the lake itself. The following morning when the local people looked out they saw a 3 mile length of water - today the lake is 5 miles long. There are reports that when the lake is clear, buildings from the old village can be seen beneath.

Nearby to Cywair's Well, Bala, is Caer Gai, once the site of a Roman Fort. The Fort was garrisoned from AD 75-130 and contained a civil settlement and a cemetery.

The Fort was positioned on an important strategic route near sources of gold, lead and manganese. Tradition has it that it was the home of Sir Ector from the King Arthur legends and the name commemorates his son Cai Hir (Long Kay) – the Sir Kay of the romances.

We will later meet the real Cai Hir, who went by the name Cadwallon Lawhir.

Camlann

In 530 Cerdic took the Isle of Wight. In 534 he was killed by Arthur's troops.

In 537 Mordred's Brigantian troops attacked Arthur where the Guletic was at his strongest, Hadrian's Wall – Camboglanna.

In 537 Arthur was 67 year old and had delivered 20 years of peace from the Saxons. Cerdic, Morded and Amhar were another matter however.

The wall had been the stronghold of Coel, Ceneu, Mar and Arthur, and it was known as the seat of the Guletic (Gwledig/warleader).

For Mordred to challenge Arthur on his home territory showed great confidence, or perhaps Arthur's troops were scattered, fighting Cerdic in the south.

Arthur's last battle, where he was fatally wounded, is not mentioned by Nennius. It is known to us from the Annales Cambriae as:

"The Strife of Camlann in which Arthur and Medraut perished".

The first mention of the Camboglanna fort is contained within the Notitia Dignitatum, the 'Register of Dignitaries' of the late-4th/early-5th centuries. In this document the Birdoswald fort is listed as Amboglanna, between the entries for Magnis (Carvoran, Northumberland) and Petrianis (Stanwix, Cumbria).

The fort is also mentioned in the seventh century Ravenna Cosmology, where it is seemingly listed twice; the first and most likely entry is named Gabaglanda, and occurs between Magnis (Carvoran, Northumberland) and Vindolande (Chesterholm, Northumberland), whereas the second entry Cambroianna, is listed between the unidentified stations Locatreve and Smetri.

The accepted name Camboglanna is Celtic in origin and translates as 'the Crooked Glen', which refers, no doubt, to the fort's spectacular southern aspect overlooking a convoluted meander of the River Irthing, towards the Roman signal station at Upper Denton on the Stanegate.

There are sixty-two inscribed stones recorded for Birdoswald, comprising: forty-four altars and other votive stones, ten building inscriptions, cohort and centurial stones, four tombstone and four other indesignated texts. These include fifteen inscriptions, all dateable to the third century.

A large civil settlement has long been known to exist in the area to the immediate south-west of the fort.

The burial ground at Birdoswald has also been identified in the area to the south-east of the fort, close to the edge of the Irthing escarpment. The reason why the burial ground lay so far away from the vicus had been a complete mystery for quite some time, until in 1999, the site was visited by a group of archaeologists operating under the electronic eyes of Channel 4's The Time Team.

Birdoswald stands high above a meander in the River Irthing, in one of the most picturesque settings on Hadrian's Wall. A Roman fort, turret and milecastle can all be seen on this excellent stretch of the Wall.

With probably the best-preserved defences of any Wall fort, this was an important base for some 1,000 Roman soldiers, succeeding an earlier fort of turf and timber. The section of Wall to the east, also of stone replacing turf, is the longest continuous stretch visible today.

Archaeological discoveries over the past 150 years have revealed a great deal about Roman military life at Birdoswald. Three of the four main gateways of the fort have been unearthed, as have the outside walls, two granary buildings, workshops and a unique drill hall.

People continued to live at Birdoswald after the Roman withdrawal. In the 5th century a large timber hall was built over the collapsed Roman granaries, perhaps for a local British chieftain. Later, a medieval tower house was raised here, replaced in the 16th century by a fortified 'bastle' farmhouse designed to protect its inhabitants from the notorious 'Border Reivers'. Later still, in more peaceful times, a farmhouse stood here.

The Birdoswald Visitor Centre provides a good introduction to Hadrian's Wall, and tells the intriguing story of Birdoswald and the people who have lived here over the past 2,000 years. Maybe the legends are correct. Maybe Queen Cywair (Gwenhwyfar) and Arthur's most trusted brother Llaenauc (Lancelot) did have an adultrous affair - this we are hardly likely to find out. But we do know she later became regarded as a Saint, just like the Guinevere of legend became a nun. Either way, when Arthur, the unbeatable warlord, rode into battle at Camboglanna, something was different. Perhaps the King was now too old. Perhaps having to kill his own brother Cerdic and his own son Amhar was enough to break him. Perhaps he and his warriors riding into battle along Hadrian's Wall, where his ancestor Artorius Castus had fought, made this all too ominous for Arthur.

Mordred was killed and his son Madog took up command. Perhaps like Artorius Castus and like the Sarmatian legend of Batraz, Arthur passed his sword to one of his warriors and told him to throw it into the water.

King Arthur, Dux Bellorum, Guletic, Pendragon, Ameradawr, Imperator, Emperor and King of Britain, fell ill and abdicated his kingdom.

Standing stones near Coventina's Well, Hadrian's Wall

Eda and Ida

According to the Harleian manuscripts it was Eda Elyn Mawr who delivered the fatal blow to Arthur. Eda is listed as the grandson of Alla and therefore they correspond with the Angle dynasty of Aelle and Ida.

And Ida we know ruled in Northumberland from the 540s, confirming it was Arthwys he succeeded.

The Lady in the Lake

In Arthurian legend, Excalibur was thrown in the water for Vivianna (the Lady in the Lake). The real Vivianna (not to be confused with St Nyfaine the real Nimue) was the goddess Covianna or Coventina.

Roman and British soldiers would throw swords and coins as offerings to her. And if Arthur was mortally wounded and gave up his sword at Camboglanna, then Coventina's well nearby would be the fitting location.

Coventina was a Romano-British goddess of wells and springs. She is known from multiple inscriptions at one site in the Northumberland County of the United Kingdom, an area surrounding a wellspring near Carrawburgh on Hadrian's Wall.

Dedications to Coventina and votive deposits were found in a walled area which had been built to contain the outflow from a spring now called "Coventina's Well". The well and the walled area surrounding it are nearby the site variously referred to as Procolita, Brocolitia, or Brocolita, once a Roman fort and settlement on Hadrian's Wall, now known as Carrawburgh.

Excavation also revealed a large quantity of coinage, from early Augustan coins to those of the late 4th century, and other votive objects such as brooches, rings, pins, glassware, and pottery. These are assumed to be votive offerings due to the quantity discovered in a single location.

Avalon and "Glastonbury"

Near to Camboglanna was another fort on Hadrian's Wall called Aballana, later Avallana. It was dedicated to Latis, Goddess of Lakes. This was where Arthur was taken to have his wounds tended.

While the Arthurian legends state Arthur's resting place was "Avalon" they also identify this place with Glastonbury.

From the real Avalon, Avallana, Arthur was laid to rest at Whithorn, the Saxon name of which was Witrin Burgh or Glas Bury. Nearby to this site are two places of immediate interest to Arthurian studies – the Mote of Mark, and St Ninian's Cave. Here we have King Arthur, King Mark and Ninian – the Lady of the Lake at the same resting place.

So now we know that Arthwys fought his last battle at Hadrian's Wall (Camboglanna) and we can see that his Lady of the Lake, Avalon and Glasto were there too.

After his injuries he returned to Wales, as we see from his wife Cywair (Gwenhwyfar), friend Cai (Cadwallon) and advisor Myrddin Emrys (Pabo) all making their home there. And it is in Wales we find the likely grave of Arthwys of Elmet:

The grave of Arthur?

In Gwynedd there was even a plaque that could mark the resting place of Arthur of Elmet. It states:

ALIORTUS ELMETIACO HIC IACET
Here lies Aliortus of Elmet

In the Book of Taliesin, Arthur is referred to as Alator – thereby comparing him to the celtic god of that name. It states that Teyrnon ("great lord"), is said to be "of the lineage of Aladur" (o echen Aladur).

This stone was found in 1865 in a field opposite the church called Gardd Sant (Erw Sant today). It can be seen on the wall of the north transept within the church. It dates to the 5th or 6th century.

Royal Commission on the Ancient and Historical Monuments for Wales entry on the stone:

Map Reference: SH34SE
Grid Reference: SH38704482
Unitary (Local) Authority: Gwynedd Old County:
Caernarfonshire
Community: Llanaelhaearn
Type of Site: INSCRIBED STONE
Broad Class: Commemorative
Period: Medieval
A roughly hewn pillar stone, 1.37m by 0.32m, inscribed vertically:
ALIORTVS ELMETIACO/HIC IACET

-thought to signify 'Aliortus of Elmet lies here'. Elmet was an early medieval polity in the area of southern Yorkshire. The inscription is thought to date to the 5th or early 6th century AD. Found when extending the churchyard and reset within the north trancept of church in about 1865. Could this explain why Arthur's grave was such a wonder? He was simply buried with his name and title - Arthur of Elmet.

Sir Melwas-Maleagant

While Arthur may have wanted to be succeeded by his son Keidyaw, Maelgwyn Gwynedd had other ideas.

He murdered his uncle Owain Ddantgwyn for Powys, took his father Cadwallon's Gwynedd and when Arthur abdicated he was made Pendragon.

The Mostyn MS117 states: Maelgwyn Gwynedd was elected King of the Island of Britain after Arthur.

Taliesin states: Be neither blessing nor success to Malegwyn Gwynedd. May vengeance overtake him for the wrongs, the treachery and the cruelty he has shown to the Race of Arthur.

Sir Cador: Successor of Arthur

In the Arthurian legends, Arthur passed his throne to Constantine, son of Cador.

In 540 Arthur was still alive and suffering from his injuries. He passed overall leadership to his son Keidyaw, the King Cador of legend, and many of his legions to his other son Eleuther who he perhaps called Uther II. But there were other claimants to Arthur's throne.

In Bernicia the Saxon leader Ida was advancing and gaining ground. In Gwynedd, King Maelgwyn had started referring to himself as the Pendragon.

Arthur's former charioteer Cuneglas succeeded his father Owain and was the most influential king in the Powys-Rhos region and a king calling himself Aurelius Conan - no doubt to draw comparisons with Ambrosius Aurelianus. And of course Cerdic's sons Cynric and Creoda (Cawrdaf) still had designs on expanding their father's kingdom of Wessex.

Even with the abdication of Arthur, Britain it seemed was still at Civil War and in Civil War what chance did it have against the invading Saxons...

Saint Gildas (c.500 – c. 570) was a prominent member of the Celtic Christian church in Britain, whose renowned learning and literary style earned him the designation Gildas Sapiens (Gildas the Wise).

Gildas' surviving written work, De Excidio et Conquestu Britanniae or On the Ruin and Conquest of Britain, is a sermon in three parts condemning the acts of his contemporaries, both secular and religious. The first part consists of Gildas' explanation for his work and a brief narrative of Roman Britain from its conquest under the principate to Gildas' time:

In the second part, opening with the assertion "Britain has kings, yet they are tyrants; it has judges, yet they are undutiful", Gildas addresses the lives and actions of five contemporary rulers: Constantine of Dumnonia, Aurelius Caninus, Vortiporius of the Demetae (now called Dyfed), Cuneglasus apparently of Powys and lastly Maglocunus or Maelgwn.

In De Excidio et Conquestu Britanniae, Gildas seems to mention that the year of his birth was the same year that the Battle of Mons Badonicus took place. The Annales Cambriae gives the year of his death as 570; however the Annals of Tigernach date his death to 569.

Gildas would have known Arthur or at least known of him. He is our primary source for some of the men that followed Arthur. But as we know from later stories, they were not Arthur's immediate successors.

Cador, it seems, was Arthur's main successor as far as being a King of Britain, and is undoubtably the Sir Cador of Arthurian mythology. Cador appears in Geoffrey of Monmouth's History of the Kings of Britain (1136) where we are told he was of Roman stock.

At the great Siege of Mount Badon, Sir Cador commanded the British contingent that chased the invaders back to their boats at Thanet, where he killed their king, Cheldric. He took part in further campaigns against the Scots at Loch Lomond and the

Gauls & Romans on the Continent. Together with Sir Lancelot, he was responsible for holding off an ambush by the Roman Emperor when taking prisoners back to Paris; and he commanded the rear guard at the Battle of Soissons.

King Arthur's other son and successor as leader of the armies of the North was Eleuther or Eliffer Gosgorddfawr - of the Great Army - (Llacheu of legend) he took his epithet from his armed followers who were legendary throughout Britain in the mid-6th century. They were thought to be unbeatable when allied to the armies of Rheged and Gododdin. It was these infantry spearmen who kept the incoming Anglian settlers under control on the edge of Eleuther's territory.

Eliffer married Erfiddyl, daughter of King Cynfarch Oer of North Rheged, and they had three children: Peredur Arueu Dur, Gwrgi and Ceindrych Benasgel (the Wing-Headed). They are supposed to have been triplets.

Aneirin's Gododdin
Prince Aneirin of Flowing Verse, a younger son of King Dunaut Bwr (the Stout) of the Northern Pennines, is one of the best known of ancient Celtic bards. He was sometimes known as Aneirin Awenyd - the Inspired - and was described by his near contemporaries as High-King of Bards or Prince of Poets.

He was apparently present at the Battle of Catraeth, between a British coalition under King Mynyddog Mwynfawr (the Wealthy) of Din-Eityn and the Anglians of Northumbria. Here he wrote the now famous poem, Y Gododdin. Though the surviving text has become corrupted and added to, the core section is believed to have actually been written by this man around the year 600.

His other works are collectively known as the Llyfr Aneirin. In later life he became a monk at Llancarfan in South Wales, where he had been educated as a boy. He was apparently killed by a blow to the head inflicted by Heidyn ap Enygan and became revered by some as a saint.

The works attributed to Aneirin are preserved in a late-13th century manuscript known as the Book of Aneirin (or Llyfr Aneirin). The language has been partially modernized into

Middle Welsh, but other portions in Old Welsh indicate that at least some of the poetry dates from around Aneirin's time, and its attribution, therefore, may well be genuine. The work would have survived through oral transmission until first written down, perhaps in the 9th century.

Aneirin's best known work is Y Gododdin, a series of elegies for the warriors of the northern Brythonic kingdom of Gododdin who, in circa 600, fell against the Angles of Deira and Bernicia at the Battle of Catraeth (probably Catterick in North Yorkshire).

One stanza contains what is generally believed to be the earliest reference to his kinsman King Arthur as a paragon of bravery, with whom one fallen warrior is compared.

The poem tells us that Aneirin was present at this battle and, having been taken prisoner, was one of only four (or two) Brythonic survivors. He remained a captive until his ransom was paid by Ceneu ap Llywarch Hen.

The stanzas which make up the poem are a series of elegies for warriors who fell in battle against vastly superior numbers. Some of the verses refer to the entire host, others eulogize individual heroes. They tell how the Gododdin king, Mynyddog Mwynfawr, gathered warriors from several Brythonic kingdoms and provided them with a year's feasting and drinking mead in his halls at Din Eidyn, before launching a campaign in which almost all of them were killed fighting against overwhelming odds.

The poetry is based on a fixed number of syllables, though there is some irregularity, which may be due to modernisation of the language during oral transmission. It uses rhyme, both end-rhyme and internal, and some parts use alliteration. A number of stanzas may open with the same words, for example "Gwyr a aeth gatraeth gan wawr" ("Men went to Catraeth at dawn").

The collection appears to have been compiled from two different versions: according to some verses there were 300 men of the Gododdin, and only one, Cynon fab Clytno, survived; in others there were 363 warriors and three survivors, in addition to the poet, who as a bard would have almost certainly not have been counted as one of the warriors. The names of about eighty warriors are given in the poem.

The Book of Aneirin begins with the introduction Hwn yw e gododin. aneirin ae cant ("This is the Gododdin; Aneirin sang it"). The first stanza appears to be a reciter's prologue, composed after the death of Aneirin:

Gododin, gomynaf oth blegyt
yg gwyd cant en aryal en emwyt:
Er pan want maws mur trin,
er pan aeth daear ar Aneirin,
nu neut ysgaras nat a Gododin.

Gododdin, I make claim on thy behalf In the presence of the throng boldly in the court:
Since the gentle one, the wall of battle, was slain, Since earth covered Aneirin, Poetry is now parted from the Gododdin.

Mead is mentioned in many stanzas, sometimes with the suggestion that it is linked to their deaths. This led some 19th century editors to assume that the warriors went into battle drunk, however "mead" here stood for everything the warriors received from their lord. In return, they were expected to "pay their mead" by being loyal to their lord unto death.

Many personal names are given, but only two are recorded in other sources. One of the warriors was Cynon fab Clytno, the other is Arthur. If the mention of Arthur formed part of the original poem this could be the earliest reference to Arthur as a paragon of bravery. In stanza 99, the poet praises one of the warriors, Gwawrddur:

He fed black ravens on the rampart of a fortress - Though he was no Arthur - Among the powerful ones in battle - In the front rank, Gwawrddur was a palisade

The poem is set in the area which is now southern Scotland and north-east England. Around the year 600 this area included a number of Brythonic kingdoms. Apart from the Gododdin, the kingdom of Alt Clut occupied the Strathclyde area and Rheged covered parts of Galloway and Cumbria. Further south lay the kingdom of Elmet in the Leeds area. These areas made up what was later known in Welsh as Yr Hen Ogledd (The Old North).

The Gododdin, known as the Votadini in the Romano-British period, occupied a territory from the area around the head of the Firth of Forth as far south as the River Wear. In modern terms their lands included much of Clackmannanshire and the Lothian and Borders regions.

Their capital at this period was probably Din Eidyn, now known as Edinburgh. By this time the area that later became Northumbria had been invaded and increasingly occupied by the Anglo-Saxon kingdoms of Deira and Bernicia.

The battle at Catraeth has been seen as an attempt to resist the advance of the Angles, who had probably by then occupied the former Votadini lands of Bryneich in modern north-eastern England and made it their kingdom of Bernicia.

At some time after the battle, the Angles absorbed the Gododdin kingdom, possibly after the fall of their capital Din Eidyn in 638, and incorporated it into the kingdom of Northumbria.

Galahad in the Gododdin

There are two surviving poems in praise of King Llaenawc of Elmet's son, Gwallawc the Battle Horseman, and it is one of these that identifies the Kingdom which was ruled by his line. In En env Gvledic nef gorchordyon, he is called "a judge over Elmet".

Gwallawc's reign was at its height in the late 6th century, when he allied himself to his cousin, Urien Rheged, and his confederation of British Kings, which included Kings Morcant Bulc of Bryneich and Riderch Hael of Strathclyde. Together, they caused much discomfort to King Hussa of Bernicia and his men. Gwallawc was present at the Siege of Ynys Metcaut, against him, in 590. It is thought he may have contributed a sea-faring contingent to the coalition.

The Battle for Arthur's Crown

The site of the Battle of Arthuret

In 540AD King Arthur died. Seven years later and ten years after the Battle of Camlann, the Kings of Britain were still at odds over dominance of the country.

Welsh sources say Arthur was killed by Eda Elleyn Mawr. Nennius states that after Arthur died, Ida became king in the North – further proof, if it were needed, that Arthur was Arthwys of the Pennines.

According to the "Veritas Historia De Mortii Athurii" Arthur won the Battle of Camlan, and, wounded, sat down and began to remove his armour. Eda Elleyn Mawr rode up on horseback and fatally injured him with a thrown spear dipped in adder's venom.

Nennius states: *"The twelfth battle was on Mount Badon in which there fell in one day 960 men from one charge by Arthur; and no one struck them down except Arthur himself, and in all the wars he emerged as victor.*

"And while they were being defeated in all the battles, they were seeking assistance from Germany and their numbers were being augmented many times over without interruption. And they brought over kings from Germany that they might reign over

them in Britain, right down to the time in which Ida reigned, who was son of Eobba. He was the first king in Bernicia, i.e., in Berneich.

The battle lines are drawn

As the 550s moved into the 560s a new generation of warrior emerged - a generation that did not have first hand memory of Arthur, Ambrosius and Uther - an ambitious generation that wanted to make a name for itself. Kings married princesses and princes formed allegiances with warlords. The battle lines were being to drawn to decide who would be the dominant Celtic king to repel the Saxon threat. Across the north three alliances were forged:

Eleuther's Great Retinue

King Eleuther and his sons Prince Peredur (Sir Perceval) and Prince Gurci
who opposed...

The House of Camulod

King Keidyaw, his son Prince Gwenddolau
King Madog and his son Myrdinn
King Gabran of Dalriada and his son Prince Aedan
who opposed...

The House of Rheged

King Cinmarc and his son Urien King Rhyderrerch and Clydno
King Gwalawg of Elmet

What is interesting - if not surprising - is the relationship that most of the antagonists have/had with the real King Arthur. Eleuther was his son and Peredur and Gurci therefore his grandchildren Keidyaw was his son and Gwenddolau therefore his grandson. Madog was the son of Morydd and therefore the nephew of Arthur, making his son Myrdinn Arthur's great-nephew. Cinmarc was a cousin of Arthur, as his father

Meirchionn was the nephew of Arthur's father. Gwallawg was the son of Llaenawc and therefore the nephew of Arthur

Sir Perceval

At the iconic closing credits of Boorman's Excalibur, Sir Perceval was seen throwing Excalibur to the Lady of the Lake as Arthur sailed away to Avalon. It is interesting imagery since two generations after Arthur's death it was the real Peredur who had the best claim to be Pendragon of Britain.

The one key difference between identifying Peredur with Perceval is that it is one of the few instances where everybody agrees that the mythical knight evolved from the real warrior in question.

Peredur son of Efrawg is one of the three Welsh Romances associated with the Mabinogion. It tells what is essentially the same story as Chrétien de Troyes' unfinished romance Perceval, the Story of the Grail, but it contains many striking differences from that work, most notably the absence of the French poem's central object, the Holy Grail. Peredur survives in the White Book of Rhydderch and the Red Book of Hergest, both from the 14th century.

The hero of the poem, has a father, Efrawg, whose name has been etymologically associated with York (Ebrauc) or from Eleuther.

Like the other Welsh Romances, scholars debate as to the work's exact relationship to Chrétien's poem. It is possible Peredur preserves some of the material found in Chrétien's source.

As Arthwys was a Romanised leader at Hadrian's Wall it may be that Peredur was derived from Praetor (praetorian prefect.)

His father Eleutherius (meaning Liberator) may have commanded the sixth legion (the 'great retinue').

The sequence of some events are altered in Peredur, and many original episodes appear, including the hero's 14-year sojourn in Constantinople reigning with the Empress, which contains remnants of a sovereignty tale.

The Holy Grail is replaced with a severed head on a platter. Despite the differences, however, influence from the French romance cannot be discounted, particularly as its first part hardly matches the second.

As in Percival, the hero's father dies when he is young, and his mother takes him into the woods and raises him in isolation. Eventually he meets a group of knights and determines to become like them, so he travels to King Arthur's court. There, he is ridiculed by Cei and sets out on further adventures, promising to avenge Cei's insults to himself and those who defended him. While travelling he meets two of his uncles, the first plays the role of Percival's Gornemant and educates him in arms and warns him not to ask the significance of what he sees. The second replaces Chrétien's Fisher King, but instead of showing Peredur the Holy Grail he reveals a salver containing a man's severed head. The young knight does not ask about this and proceeds to further adventure, including a stay with the Nine Witches of Gloucester and the encounter with the woman who was to be his true love, Angharad Golden-Hand.

Peredur returns to Arthur's court, but soon embarks on another series of adventures that do not correspond to material in Percival.

Eventually the hero learns the severed head at his uncle's court belonged to his cousin, who had been killed by the Nine Witches. Peredur avenges his family, and is celebrated as a hero.

In later romances, his father is either King Pellinore or another worthy knight. His mother is usually unnamed but plays a significant role in the stories. His sister is the bearer of the Holy Grail, she is sometimes named Dindrane. In tales where he is Pellinore's son his brothers are Sir Tor, Sir Aglovale, Sir Lamorak, and Sir Dornar.

After the death of his father, Percival's mother takes him to the Welsh forests where she raises him ignorant to the ways of men until the age of 15.

Eventually, however, a group of knights passes through his wood, and Percival is struck by their heroic bearing. Wanting to be a knight himself, the boy travels to King Arthur's court, and after proving his worthiness as a warrior he is knighted and invited to join the Knights of the Round Table.

Even in the earliest stories he is connected to the Grail Quest. In Chrétien de Troyes' Perceval, le Conte du Graal, he meets the crippled Fisher King and sees the Holy Grail, but he fails to ask the question that would heal the injured monarch. Upon learning of his mistake he vows to find the Grail castle again and fulfill his quest.

In independent legends, supposedly the founder of the town of Pickering (North Yorks), Peredur Longspear and his twin-brother, Gwrgi - the sons of King Eliffer Gosgorddfawr - ruled Ebrauc jointly.

According to Welsh legend, their father was killed when they were still young and the Queen brought her two boys up alone. Peredur seems to have spent much of his life wreaking vengeance on his father's killers.

Peredur's lineage:
Drynwin verch vrachan mam vryen. Erduduyl gwyndorliud. Owain m vryen a morud verch vryen. Gwrgi a pheredur ac arthur penuchel a tonlut a hortnan a dyrnell trydyth gwyn dorliud.

Merlin the Wild and Sir Uriens
After Arthur and Morydd's fatal clash at Camlann it is a strange irony that their grandsons formed an alliance.

Arthur's grandson Gwendollau appointed Morydd's grandson Myrdinn as his advisor and bard. Myrdinn is responsible for one half of the legend of Merlin. Ambrosius Aurelianus/Pabo Post Prydain represent Merlin as King Arthur's military advisor and the enemy of King Vortigern. Myrdinn Caledonus gives Merlin his name, his role as a bard and soothsayer and later in life as a hermit.

The standard depiction of the character first appears in Geoffrey of Monmouth's Historia Regum Britanniae, and is based on an amalgamation of previous historical and legendary figures. Geoffrey combined existing stories of Myrddin Wyllt (Merlinus Caledonensis) with tales of Aurelius Ambrosius to form the composite figure he called Merlin Ambrosius.

The earliest (pre-12th century) Welsh poems concerning the Myrddin legend present him as a madman living a wretched existence in the Caledonian Forest, ruminating on his former existence and the disaster that brought him low: the death of his lord Gwenddoleu, whom he served as bard.

Some early references name the bard as "Lailoken"; this name especially used in the hagiography of Saint Kentigern. A version of this legend is preserved in a late 15th century manuscript, in a story called Lailoken and Kentigern. In this narrative, Kentigern meets in a deserted place with the naked, hairy madman Lailoken, also called Merlynum or "Merlin", who declares that he has been condemned for his sins to wander in the company of beasts.

He adds that he had been the cause for the deaths of all of the persons killed in the battle fought "on the plain between Liddel and Carwannok." Having told his story, the madman leaps up and flees from the presence of the saint back into the wilderness. He appears several times more in the narrative until at last he asks Kentigern for the sacrament, prophesying that he was about to die a triple death.

After some hesitation, the saint grants the madman's wish, and later that day the shepherds of King Meldred capture him, beat him with clubs, then cast him into the River Tweed where his body is pierced by a stake, thus fulfilling his prophecy.

Welsh literature has many examples of a prophetic literature, predicting the military victory of all of the Brythonic peoples of Great Britain who will join together and drive the English – and later the Normans – back into the sea. Some of these works were claimed to be the prophecies of Myrddin; some were not, as for example the Armes Prydein. This wild prophetic Merlin was also treated by Geoffrey of Monmouth in his Vita Merlini which looks like a close adaptation of a number of Myrddin poems.

King Urien of Rheged

An historical king of Rheged in northern England and southern Scotland during the 6th century. He became the 'King Urien of Gore' of Arthurian legend.

Little of Urien's history is known for sure. He was the son of a certain Cynfarch Oer and seems to have fought against the rulers of the Angle kingdom Bernicia.

Early on, the relationship between Rheged and its neighboring British kingdoms was erratic, but Urien joined with other northern princes and defeated the rising Angles in several battles. His power and his victories, including Gwen Ystrad and Alt Clut Ford, are celebrated in the Book of Taliesin, the supposed author of which served as his bard. According to the Historia Brittonum, he was assassinated at the command of his ally, Morcant Bulc, who was jealous of his success.

The Welsh Triads called him a battle leader of Britain. He had four sons, named Owain, Riwallawn, Run and Pascen, the eldest of which succeeded him.

Urien remained a popular figure in Wales over the centuries, and he and his son Owain were incorporated into Arthurian legend as it spread from Britain to continental Europe.

His kingdom was eventually transferred to the mythical land of Gore, and the Kings Lot of Lothian and Auguselus of Scotland are sometimes said to be his brothers. During the reign of Uther Pendragon he marries Arthur's sister (often Morgan le Fay, but sometimes another sister is named). He, like the kings of several other lands, initially opposes Arthur's ascendance to the throne after Uther's death. Urien and the others rebel against the young monarch, but upon their defeat, the rebels become Arthur's allies and vassals.

In the legends his marriage to Morgan is not portrayed as a happy one, however, as in one story Morgan plots to take Excalibur, kill Urien and Arthur, and place herself and her lover Accolon on the throne. He is always said to be the father of Ywain (Owain), and many texts give him a second son, Ywain the Bastard, fathered on his seneschal's wife. The Welsh attribute to him a daughter named Morvydd.

Urien's power-base was at Caer-Ligualid (Carlisle), though he also had a palace at Llwyfenydd on the River Lyvennet, and probably at Caer-Brogwm (Brougham) and Pen Rhionydd (possibly near Stranraer) too. The heart of his kingdom was modern Cumbria, which even today is named after the British Cymri, though his Kingdom, at one time, was said to have stretched as far north as Murief (Moray).

558 - Death of King Gabhran (Sir Gawain) of Dalriada, possibly in battle. He is succeeded by his nephew, Conall mac Comgall. The Scots become subject to Pictish overlordship.

565 - King Riderch Hael of Strathclyde mounts an unsuccessful revenge attack on King Rhun Hir of Gwynedd. Rhun marches on Strathclyde and reinforces the armies of his half-brother, Bruide ipe Maelchon, in Pictland.

569 - Prince Aedan mac Gabhran of Dalriada establishes himself, in the right of his mother, as King of Manau Gododdin, with his capital at Eperpuill (Aberfoyle).

570 - Death of St. Gildas at Llantokay (Street). He is buried at Glastonbury Abbey.

c.570-75 - The Northern British Alliance is forged between the kingdoms of Strathclyde, North Rheged, Ebrauc and Elmet. They fight the Northumbrians at the Battles of Gwen Ystrad and the Cells of Berwyn.

In 573AD King Arthur's grandsons Peredur and Gwrgi of Ebrauc along with Kings Dunaut Bwr of the Northern Pennines and Riderch Hael of Strathclyde marched north to claim the fort at Caer-Laverock from King Gwenddoleu of Caer-Wenddoleu.

The latter was killed in the Battle of Arderydd (Arthuret) and his bard, Myrddin, is forced to flee into the Caledonian Forest.

From an Arthurian point of view, even though this battle took place 40 years after Arthur's death, it holds special significance: For it was an alliance essentially between Sir Perceval, Sir Galahad and Sir Uriens' men which defeated an army led by the king who was advised by Merlin and who was allied to the son of Sir Gawain.

After the battle, Merlin II was said to have gone mad and ran into the Caledonian forest to become a hermit.

After Arthuret, Gwallawg and Urien became especially powerful causing constant harassment to King Hussa of Bernicia and his men. Gwallawc was present at the Siege of Ynys Metcaut, against him, in 590. It is thought he may have contributed a sea-faring contingent to the coalition.

Pushed back to the sea's edge, the British besieged them on Ynys Metcaut (Lindisfarne) for three days, while Irish allies, under King Fiachna of Ulster, ousted the Saxons from Din-Guardi (Bamburgh).

However, before Urien could seize victory and finally rid Britain of the Saxon scourge, he himself was treacherously assassinated at Aber Lleu (Ross Low). His assassin, a nocturnal foreigner by the name of Llofan Llaf Difo (Severing-Hand), cut-off Urien's head at the instigation of the King's own ally, Morcant. The latter was, apparently, jealous of Urien's victories, and thought that he should lead the push to rid his own kingdom of the Saxon menace. His plan, of course, completely backfired and the Saxons soon re-asserted their stranglehold on the North. Urien was succeeded by his son, Owein.

The eldest son of King Urien of North Rheged, Owein was a giant of a man, best known for his association with High-King Arthur, at whose court he is said to have spent much of his youth. This, however, was after initial rivalry between the two. Peace only followed a fierce battle between them described in the Dream of Rhonabwy.

Here Owein and Arthur played Gwyddbwyll, an ancient form of chess, while their armies fought on the field of battle. Owein's Ravens, as his mounted followers were called, were nearly defeated until their King raised his flag and encouraged them to fight on with renewed vigour. After Arthur's defeat, Owein agreed to lead the High- King's own warband. Owein's ravens are remembered in his coat of arms, still used by some of his supposed descendants today.

Owein is the literary hero of one of Chrétien de Troyes' best-known works, Yvain, which was based on the old Welsh poem,

Iarlles y Ffynnawn. It tells of his adventures in Brittany, including the usual maiden rescues and fights with dragons and giants.

More mundane reality reveals Owein's role at his father's side defending the borders of their Kingdom, notably at the Battle of Argoed Llwyfain (Leeming Lane, Yorks) where he killed the great King Theodoric Fflamddwyn (the Firebrand) of Bernicia. After his father's assassination, in 590, Owein only managed to hang onto his Kingdom for a few years and soon his alliance with Gwallawg too fell apart.

Ever since Arthur's death the Britons prophesied that Arthur would come again, and for the last 1500 years royals have been given the name Arthur as a first or middle name in an effort to fulfil this prophesy.

In about 560AD, Aedan Mac Gabran, son of the Sir Gawain of legend, named his newborn son Arthur. Prince Arthur died in 584 at Scotland. He was killed in a battle against the Maetea Picts near Catterick which was won by his father, Aedan. Prince Arthur never lived to be crowned King Arthur II. He was outlived by his father who died in 604.

There are some arguments that the life of this young prince may have contributed to the legends of King Arthur, but I can find no evidence that any of Arthur of the Pennines' exploits (who, lest we forget, lived at precisely the correct time to be the Arthur) could be attributed to Prince Arthur of Dalriada.

Of course this Prince Arthur may lived too late to be "the" Arthur, and he may have fought the wrong enemies. From the earliest accounts, Arthur's chief enemies were the Saxons, not the Picts, and Áedán fought the Northumbrians after his son's death, so any suggestion that Aedan retired and abdicated his throne is false.

If Prince Arthur of Dalriada was not to be the successor of King Arthur of the Pennines, it seems we would have to wait a little longer.

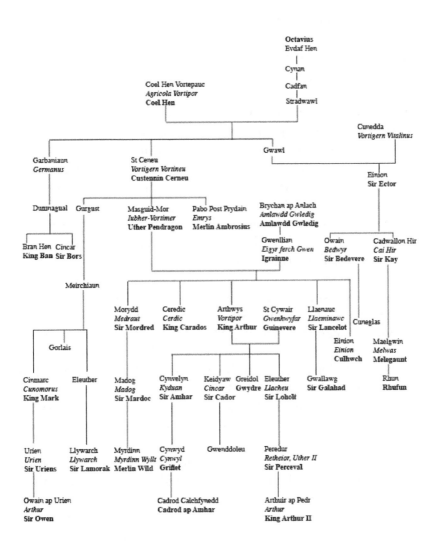

Full family tree of the real King Arthur

Legacy of Arthwys

In Book One we have discovered the true Arthur. We have discovered the historic warlord who defeated the Saxons and who inspired the legends of King Arthur.

Coel Hen was Dux of Britain, defending the northern part of the Roman Empire (marked by Hadrian's Wall) like his ancestor Artorius Castus.

Coel's son Ceneu was one of a confederation of kings who made the foolish mistake of inviting the Saxons to Britain.

Thereafter Ceneu's sons Pabo and Mar found themselves fighting these Angles and Saxons. Pabo leading the Ambrosii as Pillar of Britain and Mar ruling from the city of the legions that was York.

Mar's son Arthwys, invoking the name of Artorius Castus and the Celtic deity Artaius (the Roman Mercury), followed in the footsteps of his famous ancestors.

As Dux he defeated the Angles and subdued Scots/Picts in 12 great battles. Arthwys therefore was the Arthur we meet in histories like Nennius and the Annales Cambrae. This Arthwys had brothers called Llaenauc, Morydd, Cerdic and Einion and they formed the basis of Arthur's earliest warriors Llwch, Medraut, Caradoc and Culhwch who appeared in the earliest folk tales. Arthwys therefore was the Arthur we meet in mythology like the Mabinogion. In Arthwys ap Mar, we have almost the complete King Arthur. The Arthur hinted at in history and celebrated in folklore.

The Britain that Arthur ruled was in effect a vertical corridor. If we draw a vertical line down the middle of England this is roughly how the country was partitioned. The Angles, Saxons, Jutes and Frisians had conquered the East of the country and leaders like Arthur controlled the West. It was comparatively easy for a warleader like Arthur to travel from Carlisle to Cornwall whereas travelling from Cornwall to London was not so easy.

We know from Book One that Arthur defended the Northern Frontier of Britain along Hadrian's Wall and we also know he defended the Eastern Frontier against the Angles.

In The Peerage Of England, Or A Genealogical And Historical Account Of All The Families Of This Kingdom, That Have Born The Dignity Of Peerage, Either By Tenure, Summons To Parliament, Investiture, Or Creation, & C. From The Conquest To This Present in 1709 it was recorded: "Coel as a Dux held dominion over Gloucester.... Ceneu would not contend with his brother-in-law the emperor Constantine for the kingdom, but contented himself with this earldom."

It adds that Morudh (Mar) was his son and successor but also calls him one of King Arthur's supporters. And we know he was not only Arthur's supporter - he was his father!

"He had issue Arthwys father to Kynfelyn, father to Kynwid Kynwidion who had issue, Cadrod-Calch-Fynydh, Lord of Dunstable Coleshill, and E[arl] of Northampton, from whom descended as direct heir-male, the famous Owen/Tudor.."

In Book Two we will look at another hypothesis. That Arthur was also responsible for the Southern and Western Frontiers.

Could Arthur have also ruled in Wales, at the westernmost point that came under attack from Ireland?

Could Arthur therefore have ruled Dyfed?

Could Arthur have also ruled in Devon/Cornwall? Is there any evidence to suggest that Arthwys ap Mar held fortifications in Dumnonia?

King Arthur Contrasted with Arthwys ap Mar

King Arthur was born in around 470AD
Arthwys ap Mar was born in around 470AD

King Arthur was known as Arthur Pendragon
Arthwys ap Mar was known as Arthur Penuchel

King Arthur's Kingdom was centred on Camelot
Arthwys ap Mar's Kingdom was centred on Camulod

King Arthur fought at Camlann near Avalon and Vivianne's lake
Arthwys ap Mar fought at Camboglanna near Avallana and Coventina's Well

King Arthur's wife was Gwenhwyfar ferch Cynwyd who became a nun
Arthwys ap Mar's wife was Cywair who became a saint

King Arthur's kinsman was Einion (Culhwch)
Arthwys ap Mar's brother was Einion

King Arthur's commander was Llenlleawg (Lancelot father of Galahad)
Arthwys ap Mar's commander/brother was Llenauc father of Gwallawg

King Arthur's brother was Mordred
Arthwys ap Mar's brother was Morydd

King Arthur was related to Morgan, Anna and Nimue
Arthwys ap Mar was related to Madrun, Anna and Nyfaine

King Arthur's coronation was attended by Pabo and Ceneu
Arthwys ap Mar's coronation was attended by Pabo and Ceneu (his uncle and grandfather would surely have attended if alive)

King Arthur was the grandfather of Cadrod Calchfynedd
Arthwys ap Mar was the great grandfather of Cadrod Calchfynedd

King Arthur's successor was Cador's son
Arthwys ap Mar's successor was Keidyaw

King Arthur was the father of Gwydre
Arthwys ap Mar was the father of Greidol whose son was Gwythre

King Arthur's father was Iubher (Uther) who ruled in York (Iubher)
Arthwys ap Mar's father ruled in York (Iubher)

King Arthur's uncle was Count of Britain
Arthwys ap Mar's uncle was Father and Pillar of Britain

King Arthur's paternal grandfather was St Custennin
Arthwys ap Mar's paternal grandfather was St Ceneu

King Arthur's maternal grandfather was Amladd
Arthwys ap Mar's maternal grandfather was Brychan ap Amlach

King Arthur's kingdom was lost to Eda Elyn Mawr
Arthwys ap Mar's kingdom was lost to Ida

King Arthur's 12 battles were mostly, or entirely fought in the North
Arthwys ap Mar's battles were mostly, or entirely fought in the North

King Arthur was mentioned by Aneirin and Taliesin
Arthwys ap Mar was related to Aneirin and Taliesin

King Arthur was related to Sir Uriens
Arthwys ap Mar was related to Urien Rheged

King Arthur was related to King Mark (Cunomorus)
Arthwys ap Mar was related to Cinmarc ap Meirchion

King Arthur's kingdom was near that of Tristan
Arthwys ap Mar's kingdom was near that of Drustan

King Arthur was closely linked to Myrdinn
Arthwys ap Mar was closely related to Myrdinn

King Arthur was closely linked to Peredur
Arthwys ap Mar was closely related to Peredur

King Arthur was descended from Evdaf
Arthwys ap Mar was descended from Evdaf

King Arthur had a son named Kyduan
Arthwys ap Mar had a son named Kynvelin

King Arthur won the battle of Badon
Arthwys ap Mar's kingdom included Batham (Buxton) - a Roman bath town.

Arthwys ap Mar: The Once and Future King
The more we look at Geoffrey of Monmouth in the light of discovering Arthwys ap Mar was King Arthur, the more we see that Geoffrey was telling the truth about working from an "ancient book".

It is often assumed that Geoffrey worked only from sources like Gildas, Nennius and Culhwch and invented the rest but this is simply not likely.

As Gidlow point out, Geoffrey knows about Camlan, but is unlikely to know about it from the Annales Cambrae. He also knows about older rulers like Cunobelinus (not documented in these books) who we only found out were real when archaeology discovered their coins.

That Geoffrey places Archgallo and Peredurus in his book shows he had access to northern pedigrees and the fact that he lists Pabo and Ceneu as having attended Arthur's coronation suggests this again. Geoffrey uses Modred rather than Medraut which is closer to Morydd.

The biggest contention about Geoffrey is that he has Arthur defeating Rome, where other medieval sources have him in civil war with Lancelot. Could Lucius Hiberius have been Lugh of Hibernia - his brother Llaenawc?

If following only Welsh sources like Culhwch, Geoffrey would not place Uther and Arthur's battles in York - yet he does.

Arthur established in history
I have demonstrated that the approximate years given in every source from the Annales Cambrae to Thomas Mallory is correct - Mallory has the Graal quest in 487, the Annales have Badon in 516 and Camlann in 537 - so an Arthur born in around 470 could easily fight his last battle at age 67.

I have demonstrated that there are clear indications that Arthur existed:

1) Contemporary sources like Gildas cite the Battle of Badon - no other leader is ever listed as winning Badon
- The Annales Cambrae give Arthur as the winner at Badon
- Nennius gives Arthur as the winner at Badon
- Culhwch gives Arthur as the winner at Caer Faddon (Badon)
- None of these sources are directly related and have no reason to insert Arthur as the winner in place of someone else.

2) Arthur is most closely associated with York and Hadrian's Wall in early sources
- The first reference to him, the Gododdin is of North Yorkshire

- Bards like Llywarch Hen and Taliesin who are next to mention him were from the north
- Most of the battles listed by Nennius fit best in the north
- Arthur was the Dux. The Dux was always stationed in the north
- Even Geoffrey has Arthur and Uther fighting campaigns in York
- Nennius tells us about Arthur, then immediately after tells us about Ida who took the north after Arthur
- From the king lists Arthwys ap Mar is the only one of the correct age and location

3) Soon after Arthur's lifetime other kings called their sons Arthur

4) Camlann was most likely at Hadrian's Wall where Arthur commanded the 6th Legion.

And that is the Arthur of history, a prince from York who became the Dux at Hadrian's Wall. Who led the kings of Britain against the Saxons/Angles/Picts in 12 battles and fought his last at Camlann.

However we also have the Arthur of Welsh mythology. All of his early friends and foes are accounted for.

- Uther (also called Iubher) was Arthwys father Mar who ruled at Ebrauc (also called Iubher)
- Eigyr (daughter of Gwen) was Arthwys' mother Gwenllian
- Llwch Llaminauc was Arthwys' brother Llaenauc
- Culhwch (also called Einion) was Arthwys' brother Einion
- Caradoc Vreichvras was Arthwys' brother Ceredig
- Modred was Arthwys' brother Morydd
- Arthur's son Kyduan was Arthwys's son Cynvelyn
- Arthur's wife Gwenhwyfar of Ireland who was Arthwys' wife Cywair of Ireland

And we also have people who arrived later such as:

- Galahad son of Lancelot who was Gwallawg son of Llaenauc

142

- Merlin/Myrdinn who was of course Myrdinn - a member of Arthwys' family
- Perceval/Peredur - another key member of Arthwys' family
- Arthur's successor Cador who was Arthwys' son Keidyaw
- Gorlois and Mark are really Gorlais and Cinmarc, also found in the north along with Urien and Tristan.

At Hadrian's Wall we have found not only Camlann, but the real Vivianne's Lake (Coventina's well) and Avalon.

We have also found the real Caer Legion (York, the city of the last legion), the real Camelot (Camulod near York), the real Round Table and monuments to Arthur of York in both Wales and Cornwall.

PENNINE DRAGON

BOOK TWO
BEARMAN PENDRAGON

In Llongborth I saw Arthur, And brave men who hewed down with steel, Emperor, and conductor of the toll. **Llywarch Hen**

In the previous chapters I introduced the hypothesis that King Arthur should be identified with the historic Arthwys of Ebrauc (York), otherwise known as Arthwys of the Pennines. His kingdom of Camelot was really Camulod in Yorkshire. His wife Gwenhwyfar was St Cywair. And his father Uther was Mar of Ebrauc.

Along the way we encountered the real Igraine, Nimue, Morgan and Anna. We met the real Merlin and the real Lady of the Lake. We also met Lancelot, Galahad, Mordred, Cador, Gawain, Perceval and almost every other Arthurian character and they were all identified with Northern characters.

We identified 13 of Arthur's battles that all occurred in the North. But we also discovered that Arthur was a national King, a Dux Bellorum, a Pendragon. So now, with him firmly identified as a King ruling from what is now Yorkshire, we should explore the rest of his kingdom.

We will investigate the hypothesis that not only was the historic King Arthur a king of York but he actually did rule the whole kingdom of Britain with bases in York, Dyfed and Cornwall.

Ambrosius Aurelianus (Merlin Emrys): Pabo Post Prydain: The Pillar of Britain and Brittany

In book one we met Ambrosius Aurelianus, the uncle of King Arthur who was recorded by near-contemporary historians such as Gildas and Bede. While Ambrosius is well remembered in history, he is nowhere to be seen in family pedigrees. This is because he was referred to as Pabo Post Prydain (Father and Pillar of Britain) a reference to his titles Commes Brittanium (count or vicar of Britain).

In the genealogies we see Pabo (Ambrosius) was grandson of the King of Northern Britain Coel Hen, who guarded Hadrian's Wall under the last Roman governors. His father was Ceneu, and his brothers Germanus and Mar (Uther).

147

But could Pabo Post Prydain, a man whose power base was York, Leeds and the Pennines, have also held influence as far south as Cornwall (then called Kernow, part of Dumnonia) and even across the sea to Brittany (then called Armorica)? This answer, it would seem, is yes. In around 470 Pabo succeeded the legendary Riothamus as commander of the Britons on the continent. In Cornwall and Brittany, Pabo was called, rather fittingly Pabo the Royal.

In his book, King Arthur: The Truth Behind the Legend, Rodney Castleden relates:

"We hear of a King called Riwal ('Royal') who apparently was known in the first half of the sixth century by his Latin name, Pompeus Regalis, **so his Celtic name must have been Pabo**. He was a relative of Gereint and Cadw and 'chief on both sides of the sea': in other words he held lands in both Dumnonia and Brittany."

Pabo Riwal Mawr Marchou (Pabo the Great Royal Knight) as he was known across the sea is said to have hailed from Britain and to have migrated to Brittany with a large number of followers.

Riwal found it politic to pay homage to the king of the Franks, as well as his cousins in Cornouaille, in order to secure his position.

When Prince Fracan of Cerniw settled in Domnonée, he quickly had a set-to with his new monarch. Riwal claimed to have a much swifter horse than Fracan, but the latter could not agree. They organised a race to decide whose beast was the best, but the new arrival's jockey fell and was nearly killed. Luckily, Fracan's son, St. Winwaloe was able to heal him. Riwal may have been impressed by this saint's miracle working for he became a patron of the church and gave much land to his cousin, St.Brioc.

Riwal is recorded to have probably died around AD 520, but actually we know Pabo died in around 530.

In Britain, Pabo the Royal was referred to by his Roman title Ambrosius Aurelianus as he commanded units called the Ambrosiaci. These garrisons surrounded the old territory of the Dobunni which was known as Calchvynedd in the Dark Ages.

However it has been argued that Calchfynedd was also the name of Kelso near Hadrian's Wall.

Morris (1973: 100) speculates that the Ambros place-names represent the locations of garrisons of Ambrosiaci, military units raised by an Ambrosius. Recent analysis of these place-names has concluded that a derivation from the personal name Ambros is still possible, although an alternative interpretation is 'place frequented by buntings'.

What is interesting about Pabo ruling as far south as Calchvynedd (the Cotswolds) is that Arthur of the Pennines was also a ruler of Calchvynedd, passing control of this (perhaps not through choice) to his rebellious son Cinbelin. If Cinbelin ruled the Ambrosiaci it further strengthens the theory that Cinbelin was the Amr (Amhar) of legend.

Cinbelin's son Cynwyd Cynwydion ruled the Leicester area as well (Caer-Lerion or Cynwydion), married Peren, the daughter of Arthur's other son Greidal (Gwydre) and their son Cadrod became the famous king Cadrod of Calchvynedd.

The British armies of Calchfynedd were defeated by King Cuthwulf of Wessex, in AD 571, at the Battle of Bedford. However, the West Saxons did not settle very deep into this British territory for some generations and the Calchfynedd dynasty probably survived for a time.

Late descriptions of Cadrod describe him as 'Earl of Dunstable' and 'Lord of Northampton' and show that it was generally thought that he lived in the Chilterns, which may take their name from Calchvynedd.

Uther Pendragon Mar of Armorica

Geoffrey of Monmouth's Uther Pendragon is also referred to as Uther Ben. In Ireland, Uther is referred to as both Iubher and Ur. It is possible then that Uther could at some point been referred to as Ur-Ben.

In book one we discovered that the name Iubher is cognate with Ebrauc (York) and this is the origin of Uther's name, and for sure we discovered that the real Uther Pendragon, was the father of Arthur of the Pennines, King Mar of York. But could it be possible that Mar, like his brother Pabo (Ambrosius Aurelianus) ruled not only in York, but also in Cornwall and in Brittany. Could it be possible that Mar was referred to as Ur- Ben or Erbin?

It may seem strange to the reader that one person could have so many spellings of their name. Some may think that Arthur, Artur, Artuir, Arthwys, Arthuis, Athrwys and Artorius could not possibly be the same for instance - but 1,500 years ago there was no standard for spelling.

Uther's story is first told by Geoffrey of Monmouth in his "History of Kings of Britain" where he is a son of King Constantine Waredwr (actually we have seen he was the son of Ceneu not Constantine).

Constantine's son in Gereint and Enid is Erbin. Could this Erbin be Ur-Ben, Uther Pendragon? This would further explain why Uther was inserted into a Cornish genealogy.

The kings of York, Dyfed and Dumnonia shown with the legendary Arthurian kings:

High Kings of the North	Kings of Dyfed	Kings of Dumnonia	Legendary Arthurian Kings
Coel Hen Vortepauc	Agricola		Vortigern the Elder Ambrosius the Elder
Ceneu		Constantine	Vortigern
Mor	Erbin	Erbin	Vortimer Emrys & Uther
Arthwys Kynvelyn	Vortipor	Gereint	King Arthur
Keidyaw	Congair	Cador	Arthur passed his kingdom to Cador's son
Peredur	Pedr (Retheior)	Peredur	Arthur gave his sword to Bedwyr or Peredur
	Artuir		

150

The Three Kingdoms of Arthur

Arthur as Chief Prince in Mynyw, and Dewi as Chief Bishop, and Mælgwn Gwynedd as Chief Elder; Arthur as Chief Prince in Celliwig in Cerniw, and Bishop Bytwini as Chief Bishop, and Caradog Freichfras as Chief Elder; Arthur as Chief Prince in Pen Rhionydd in the North, and Gerthmwl Wledig as Chief Elder, and Cyndeyrn Garthwys as Chief Bishop.

The Welsh Triads

History records that Coel Hen of Ebrauc was the last Dux Brittanorum. His grandson Ambrosius Aurelianus was the most powerful leader in Britain and may have been the Commes Brittanorum. Ambrosius' nephew Arthur was recorded by Nennius as Dux Bellorum and led the Kings of Britain into battle.

As we saw in book one, Arthur, like his uncle and great grandfather, maintained defences along Hadrian's Wall (Camboglanna or Camlann), he held court at Ebrauc and Elmet (roughly York and Leeds) and also in the Cities of the Legions - places like Carlisle and Chester.

Arthur defeated the Saxons in 12 straight battles across what is now Northern England and Lowland Scotland. But did Arthur ever venture south? Did he, as the legends state, flourish in what is now Wales and Cornwall and Brittany? I believe the answer is yes. And the clues are found in the historical pedigrees.

Agricola is often thought to have lived in around 470, much later than Coel Hen, but this is because he is named prior to Vortipor in the genealogies - but some generations could be missing.

Coel Hen ruled in Ayr (now Scotland) - if he was sent to Wales surely he might be known as Ayr Coel - which would account for his name Air Coll or Agricola.

Dyfed, now Carmarthenshire, Cardiganshire, Pembrokeshire was then called Demetia after the Demetae tribe. Because west Wales faces Ireland the Irish Deissi tribe often invaded and so the

Romans protected the coast. Did Ayr Coel become the Agricola who protected Dyfed against invaders?

We have already looked into the possibility that Uther was called both Mor "sea" in the north (maybe in reference to his trips across the sea) - it seems in both Dyfed and Dumnonia he was called Erbin ("Uther Ben" or Uther Pendragon).

Of course the King Arthur of legend was Arthur of the Pennines, but spellings vary. He is sometimes recorded as Arthuis, Arthwys or even Garthwys.

When he travelled from his York "Camelot" to Dyfed he was recorded as Garthuir. A copyist error could easily write Garthuir as Gartbuir. And when Arthur's reputation as a fearsome leader developed, we can imagine the local Irish and Welsh telling him his name should be Arth (bear) or Art (stone). Could the fearsome Garthuir have taken the name Arthur in reference to his reputation as a "man of stone" or "bear-like man"?

The Expulsion of the Dessi

The Irish form is given as "Tualodor mac Rigin maic Catacuind maic Caittienn maic Clotenn maic Naee maic Artuir maic Retheoir maic Congair maic Gartbuir maic Alchoil."

We know that Vortipor, perhaps a play on the name Garthuir, is not a name - it is a title meaning 'Protector'. Could Arthur, like his great grandfather Coel, have been the Protector of the Dyfed Coast as well as Hadrian's Wall?

At the time of Arthur/Vortipor the ruler in Dumnonia is Gereint. Was Gereint one of Arthur's generals or was he Arthur himself?

- Gereint was the son of Erbin son of Constantine - Arthur was the son of Uther-Ben son of Constantine (Ceneu)

- Arthur was the father of Keidyaw - Vortipor was the father of Congair

- Keidyaw was succeeded by Peredur - Congair was succeeded by Pedr

- Gartbuir was the father of Cyngar - Gereint was the father of Cador

152

Arthur's ally in Britanny was King Hoel I. Tradition Says he was exiled to Britain where he spent his childhood in Dyfed, where he established the church of Llanhowel.

Hoel supposedly landed at Southampton and moved North to help Arthur fight at Dubglas, the Siege of Ebrauc (York) and Dunbarton. Later he joined Arthur in continental campaigns where he and Arthur ruled in Cornouaille.

Hoel, remembered as Sir Howel, died in 545 and was succeeded by his son Tewdwr Mawr who may be the same as Tewdrig of Gwent.

In Llongborth I saw Arthur, And brave men who hewed down with steel, Emperor, and conductor of the toll.
In Llongborth Geraint was slain, A brave man from the region of Dyvnaint, And before they were overpowered, they committed slaughter.

Black Book of Carmarthen

This poem suggests that Gereint and Arthur the Emperor were not the same person, if it's the case that Arthur ruled the Northern frontier, and the Dyfed frontier, perhaps Gereint ruled Dumnonia on his behalf. Perhaps he ruled as regent for Cador as well.

For this to be the case, the heroic King Arthur, who we have already identified with Arthur of the Pennines, would have to also be represented as Vortipor, protector of Dyfed. Could Arthur be the seemingly villainous Vortipor? I would suggest not but it is certainly possible.

Of course Vortipior's reputation as an evil ruler comes from Gildas, who we have already determined may not have liked Arthur (who was said to have beheaded Gilgas' brother).

Why also art thou, Vortipor, tyrant of the Demetae, foolishly stubborn? Like the leopard art thou, in manners and wickedness of various colour, though thy head is now becoming grey, upon a throne full of guile, and from top to bottom defiled by various murders and adulteries, thou worthless son of a good king, as Manasseh of Hezekiah. What! do not such wide whirlpools of sins,

*which thou suckest in like good wine, nay, art thyself swallowed
by them, though the end of life is gradually drawing near - do
these not satisfy thee? Why, to crown all thy sins, dost thou, when
thine own wife had been removed and her death had been
virtuous, by the violation of a shameless daughter, burden thy
soul as with a weight impossible to remove?"* - **Gildas**

When Gildas wrote, Arthur had all-but abdicated. He had been
mortally wounded at Camlann and was perhaps ending his days
in Dyfed. But if Arthur was born in 475 and Gildas was writing in
550, Arthur's son Cynvelyn born in around 500 could easily also
be going grey.

Gildas says of Vortipor that he is 'spotted with wickedness
like a leopard' which may suggest he was not all bad. Gildas
states that Vortipor's hair is becoming grey and that the end of
life is drawing near.

He also says that Vortipor's throne had been defined by
various murders and adulteries. Could this be the adulteries later
preserved in Arthurian legends such as between Lancelot and
Guinevere?

Could the reference to a "shameless daughter" reference
Arthur's alleged adultery with one of Guinevere's sisters or even
Arthur's own "sister" Morgan Le Fay?

Maybe Vortipor was not Arthur, rather he was Arthur's son –
the villainous Cynvelyn or Amhar, remembered in the
Dumnonian pedigrees as Kynvor, father of Constantine.

"Worthless son of a good king" would seem more befitting
Cynvelyn than Arthur - surely not even Gildas could call a man
who soundly defeated the Saxons for a generation "worthless."
Whether Vortipor is Arthwys or his son Cynvelyn, both followed
in descent from Coel (Agricola) and were related to the next in
the Dyfed succession - Congair and Pedr (Keidyaw and Peredur).
But not only do we find these Northern rulers in Dyfed - we also
find them in Cornwall.

Arthwys of Tintagel

Is Artognou descendant of Coll, the same as Arthwys descendant of Coel?

A 6th century slate inscribed with the name "ARTOGNOV", the Latin of a British name Arthnou, was discovered at Tintagel in Cornwall, the ruined castle cared for by English Heritage on behalf of the nation.

The stone bears similarities to the name of the mythical King Arthur, long associated with Tintagel. It also provides further evidence, together with other recent finds, of the existence of a possible royal site at Tintagel for the "Dark Age" rulers of Cornwall.

The "Arthur" stone and other finds were discovered just days before the latest stage of an extensive research project to reevaluate excavations before the war and the importance of Tintagel drew to a close.

The project was commissioned by English Heritage and carried out by the University of Glasgow. Dr Geoffrey Wainwright, Chief Archaeologist at English Heritage, said: "This is a find of a lifetime. It is remarkable that a stone dating from the 6th century has been discovered with the name Arthnou inscribed on it at Tintagel, a place with which the mythical King Arthur has long been associated, in a high status secular settlement.

"Despite the obvious temptation to link the Arthnou of this stone to either the historical or the legendary figure of Arthur, it must be stressed that there is no evidence to make this connection. Nevertheless, it proves for the first time that the name existed at that time and that the stone belonged to a person of status."

The slate, informally inscribed in Roman letters mainly in Latin, reads 'PATER COLIAVIFICIT ARTOGNOU' which Professor Charles Thomas, the country's leading expert on Tintagel and inscriptions of this period, suggests can be translated as 'Artognou, father of a descendant of Coll, has had (this) made/built/constructed.'

It was previously thought that Tintagel was a Celtic monastery. However, work over the previous decade and objects found during excavations in the last few years suggest that Tintagel was a high status secular site, perhaps the court of an important, if not royal, Chieftain of Dumnonia (Cornwall).

The inscription on the stone gives historians their first evidence that literacy within the ruler's circle was fairly widespread. The stone reveals that the inhabitants of Tintagel were continuing to read and write Latin and to lead a Romanised way of life long after the Romans had left England in 410AD.

Measuring about 35 cm by 20 cm, the slate has clearly been broken for re-use as a drain cover outside a 6th or 7th century building.

What could the inscriptions on the stone mean?

PATER COLIAVIFICIT ARTOGNOU
Literally: Father Coel Descendant Arth

Grammatically this could be: Arth, father of a descendant of Coel. But what if the stone refers more specifically to Arthur's ancestry: Arth, and Pabo descendants of Coel. What many translations seem to ignore however is that the stone also bears an inscription dedicated to what looks like "Maxentius". This could be either Masguid (Mar/Uther) or Magnus Maximus - who were respectively the father and great- great-great grandfather of Arthur.

Moffat states: "If that description is intended to add dignity and fame to the simple statement of Arthur's name [ie it doesn't refer to him as a king] then it can only refer to Coel Hen, the early 5th Century King of the North, a founder of the line of Rheged, perhaps the last Dux Brittanorum...

"If Arthur was a warleader whose success and expertise brought him to defend Celtic Britain, wherever it was attached then there is no doubt he came south."

In researching this book I visited a lot of Arthurian locations. From St Gildas and Huelgate in Brittany to Hadrian's Wall and York to Ruthin to Chester to Anglesey to Caldey Island to St Michael's Mount to Slaughterbridge.

And nowhere captures the myth and magic of Arthur's Britain like Tintagel castle in Cornwall. When I began to research this book many years ago I began with the assumption Arthur was born in Tintagel. Then I discovered the truth - that Arthur was a man of the York area and I was most disappointed! But as I began to research more and more I learnt that the two were not mutually exclusive.

Finding that Pabo was listed as a King in the Pennines, in Wales and in Britanny, finding that the Arthnou stone in Tintagel spoke of a "descendant of Coll", discovering the same names in the pedigrees of York, Dyfed and Dumnonia I began to understand that Arthur was not like a dark age warlord - he was more like a Roman Dux, commanding at garrisons the length of the land.

Tintagel could then be Arthur's southern base and Cadbury that of his son Cador. And Tintagel was a key location in the time Arthur was the Dux.

Just as Cornish tin was prized throughout Europe, the arts and crafts from the continent came to Britain via Cornwall. Oil jars from North Africa, globular jars from Greece, jars with foot spikes from Asia Minor, finer table pieces from western Turkey and glass from Bordeaux were all found at Tintagel. Finds came from Tunisia, Carthage and Cadiz. And as early as the 12th century Arthur was depicted on mosaics in Italy - for example Otranto Cathedral.

At the center of the Modena Archivolt image is a castle defended by two towers, inside of which are two figures identified as "Mardoc" (Madog) and "Winlogee" (Guinevere or Cywair). The left tower is defended by a pickaxe-wielding man named "Burmaltus", who faces off against Artus de Bretania (King Arthur).

On the other side, the knight "Carrado" (Carados or Cerdic?) spars with "Galvagin" (Gabran or Gawain?), while "Che" (Kay) and "Galvariun" (Gwallawg or Galahad) approach with their lances at their shoulders.

"Winlogee" most likely corresponds to Arthur's wife, Guinevere. The Abduction of Guinevere is a very popular and ancient element of the Arthurian legend, first appearing in written form in Caradoc of Llancarfan's mid-12th-century Life of Gildas. What is crucial is that these carvings pre-date the European romances of Chretien and so on. They show that the legends of Arthur were as widespread as the European trade with Tintagel. Arthur was no petty warlord of York, he was a respected Imperator whose name was known from Hadrian's Wall to Rome.

Sir Cador of Cadbury

Long after Arthur's death, the sons of his sons Keidyaw and Eleuther fought in a vicious civil war across the North of Britain. Keidyaw's son Gwendolleu (and his advisor the bard Myrdinn or Merlin) fought Eleuther's son Peredur (Sir Perceval) at the Battle of Arthuret, which also included Urien (Sir Urien) and Gwallawg (Sir Galahad).

Peredur was victorious and conquered the lands owned by Keidyaw and Gwendolleu. We know about the lands in the North but did Peredur and Keidyaw, like Arthur, Uther and Ambrosius before them, also own lands in the south? The answer is yes.

In the pedigrees of Dumnonia and Dyfed, Arthur/Vortipor/Gereint were said to have been succeeded by Cador/Cincar/Cyngar and he in turn by Peredur/Pedr/Retheior. It now becomes clear that From Coel Hen to Peredur, these men were not just kings of York, but also of the whole of Britain, sometimes Brittany and essentially head of the British Empire.

Cado appears in Arthurian literary sources as Cador, Earl of Cornwall. He is first mentioned in Geoffrey of Monmouth's History of the Kings of Britain (1136).

In fact, Cado succeeded his father, Gerren Llyngesoc (who we have already discovered was either a general of Arthur's or Arthur himself), as King of Dumnonia. His main stronghold was probably the hillfort of South Cadbury in Somerset where Leslie Alcock has excavated a sub-Roman (5th/6th century) gateway and large feasting hall. The name means "Cado's Fort" and was, no doubt, one of Cado's many palaces.

Towards the end of the 20th century many historians sought to identify Camelot (actually Camulod in Slack near York) with Cadbury and couldn't understand how something called Cado's fort could be linked with King Arthur - it is because they did not know that the real King Arthur had a son called Cador!

The travelling historian, John Leland, first recorded the association in 1542:

"Right at the South end of South Cadbury Church stands Camelot. This was once a noted town or castle, set on a real peak of a hill, and with marvellously strong natural defences... Roman coins of gold, silver and copper have been turned up in large quantities during ploughing there, and also in the fields at the foot of the hill, especially on the East side. Many other antiquities have also been found, including at Camelot, within memory, a silver horseshoe. The only information local people can offer is that they have heard that Arthur frequently came to Camelot."

Of course, Arthur came to Cadbury - it was the home of his son. Perhaps Cadbury was named for Keidyaw ap Arthwys.

Ector, Kay and Bedevere

In the Arthurian legends, Arthur is brought up in a foster family, which was very common in celtic tradition. His foster father was Sir Ector, his foster brother Sir Kay and his best friend Sir Bedevere.

Kay, or Cai Hir as he was known and Bedevere or Bedwr are among Arthur's earliest companions and join him in his adventures to the Otherworld seen in the Mabinogion. If, as we have seen, Arthur was to not only rule the North of Britain, but also Wales, it would be perfectly viable for him to be fostered somewhere other than the north - and I would suggest North Wales.

Cai Hir was Arthur's second-in-command, and at the time of the historic Arthur one of the most influential leaders was none other than Cadwallon Law Hir or - Cai Hir perhaps.

Just as Cai's father was Ector, Cadwallon's father was Einion. For Arthur to be fostered to Einion then Mar (Uther) and Einion (Ector) would have been very good friends. The fact that one of Mar's sons was called Einion (Culhwch) supports this. Cai's brother in arms was Bedwr, the historic Cadwallon's brother was Owain Ddantgwyn.

Sir Bedivere was known to the Welsh as Bedwyr Bedrydant "of the Perfect Sinews" and was therefore, presumably, a very muscular man. Along with Sir Kay alias Cai Hir (the Tall), he is one of the most ancient warriors associated with King Arthur. He appears in the Mabinogion tale of "Culhwch and Olwen" as the handsomest warrior who ever was at Arthur's Court, "and although he was one-handed no three warriors drew blood in the same field faster than he".

In the Life of St. Cadog, he was one of Arthur's entourage sent to pursue King Gwynllyw of Gwynllwg after he had abducted St. Gwladys from her father's court in Brycheiniog.

160

Bedwyr is also recorded in the Black Book of Carmarthen as having fought at the unlocated Battle of Tryfrwyd: "By the hundred they fell before Bedwyr Bedrydant" for "Furious was his nature with shield and sword".

Geoffrey of Monmouth named him as Arthur's chalice bearer, head butler and Duke of Normandy. He fought the giant of Mont St. Michel and was highly active in the King's continental campaigns, during which he may have been killed. Later literary tradition, particularly Sir Thomas Malory, makes him Sir Bedivere, the knight who returned Excalibur to the Lady of the Lake after the Battle of Camlann.

Could Bedwr have been captain of Arthur's war chariots rather than his chalice bearer? If Bedwr is, as I believe, Cai's brother Owain Ddantgwyn, then he was Arthur's charioteer as was his son Cuneglas who Gildas refers to as "Charioteer to the Bear's stronghold"

Just as the legendary Bedwr was known as "the handsomest warrior", Owain Ddantgwyn was also known for his good looks including his sparkling white teeth (Ddantgwyn means white teeth).

Welsh legend recalls an Owen Llawgoch (Red Hand) who lies sleeping in a cave - could this have been confused with Owain (Bedevere), the last knight who saw Arthur taken away to Avalon where he sleeps in a cave? Bedwyr after all means "Grave knower". The first mention of Cadwallon as Kay is in Culhwch where it is written:

Kai had this peculiarity, that his breath lasted nine nights and nine days under water, and he could exist nine nights and nine days without sleep. A wound from Kai's sword no physician could heal. Very subtle was Kai. When it pleased him he could render himself as tall as the highest tree in the forest. And he had another peculiarity - so great was the heat of his nature, that, when it rained hardest, whatever he carried remained dry for a handbreadth above and a handbreadth below his hand; and when his companions were coldest, it was to them as fuel with which to light their fire.

Pa Gur refers to Kay as a battle leader (Cadwallon means battle leader). It states: Cai the fair and Llachau, they performed battles before the pain of of blue spears (ended the conflict). The first mention of Bedevere in Culhwch states:

Arthur called upon Bedwyr, who never shrank from an enterprise upon which Cei was bound. It was thus with Bedwyr, that none was so handsome.

Cai Hir the battle leader and Cadwallon Law Hir, were the same and as Nennius stated, Arthur fought with the kings of Britain. Cai Hir was Arthur's commander just like Cadwallon Law Hir was Arthwys' commander.

King Arthur Pendragon

In these chapters we see a new vision of the Arthurian history. We begin with Coel Hen, known to the Romans as Agricola, the protector (Vortipauc) of Britain on the Northern Frontier, based at York and leading defences along Hadrian's Wall.

He is followed by his son-in-law Cunedda, appointed the Gwledig and sent to Gwynedd to defend North Wales against invasion. Meanwhile Coel's son Ceneu dealt with Saxon invasion in Bernicia. But they weren't the only ones to challenge for power. The next Gwledig was Amlach (Amlawdd Gwledig) who some say was married to Cunedda's daughter. Amlach was known as Ambrosius the Elder and he was challenged by Vortigern.

Ceneu's sons, called by the Roman factions the sons of Constantine, were Maximus Claudius (Masguid Gloff) and Ambrosius Aurelianus (Emrys Gwledig). Masguid was known as Iubher (of York), pronounced Uther and Ambrosius was known as Pabo Post Prydain, the Father and Pillar of Britain.

From the British base at Tintagel the two journeyed to Armorica (Britanny) where Pabo is remembered as Riwal and Masguid is remembered as Riothamus (Ri-Uther-Mor, perhaps King Uther of the Sea).

Arthur was crowned King of Elmet (Campudunno), Ebrauc (Camulod) and the Pennines and he set about defending northern Britain.

Defeating the Saxons in Ebrauc and Bernicia, he then sent his brother Llaenauc north of Hadrian's Wall to subdue the Picts. Arthur and Llaenauc then ventured into Irish-occupied Wales (Demetia) were they overthrew the Deissi kings and Arthur took the title Vortipor in the name of his great grandfather Agricola. Arthur joined his uncle Pabo in Cornwall and erected a stone at Tintagel reading "Arthou and Pabo, descendants of Coel built this". Arthur installed his Northern British cousin Gereint ap Erbin as commander in the south.

After Arthur's final battle at Camboglanna, his son Cador inheritted the three kingdoms. As Keidyaw he held York and also ruled from the south where his castle was called Cado's Fort (Cadbury). In Dyfed he is remembered as Congair. Cador was succeeded by in York, Dyfed and Dumnonia by his son Peredur who is the Sir Perceval of legend.

In about 1190, a burial cross apparently marking the grave of King Arthur was found in Glastonbury. It is generally dismissed as a fake, but it does include one very interesting detail:

"Here lies buried the famous King Arthurus with Wenneveria his second wife."

No other source refers to Guinevere (or variations thereof) as being Arthur's second wife, so if the cross was pure fiction, why add this detail? Did Arthur marry Cywair and then marry again, to someone called Wenneveria?

Consider Gildas' remark when he was addressing someone called Vortipor who I have theorised may have been Arthwys' title in Dyfed.

"Thy head is now becoming grey, upon a throne full of guile... Though the end of life is gradually drawing near... Why, to crown all thy sins, dost thou, when thine own wife had been removed and her death had been virtuous, by the violation of a shameless daughter."

Gildas is not accusing Vortipor of raping his own daughter (as others have suggested) he states "a daughter" which could mean any woman. And by violation, he could just mean sex before marriage or adultery.

Did Arthur remarry after Cywair died? It's a possibility. Wenneveria sounds Saxon. Was she the daughter of a Saxon enemy?

Uther as Riothamus

The identification of Riothamus with Uther was suggested by historian RW Morgan in 1848 who showed how seemlessly the story of Uther, as told by Geoffrey, fits into the life of Riothamus. He wrote:

"The Roman emperor Anthemius requesting aid from Uthyr against Euric, king of the Visigoths, Uthyr landed at Havre, at the head of 12,000 men, (A.D. 470). An engagement took place, but the Roman proconsul failing to effect a junction, Uthyr was obliged to yield the field and retire into Burgundy. Advantage was taken of his absence by Octa and Ebusa, to raise the standard of rebellion. On his return Uthyr was discomfited by them at York, but afterwards defeated and took them prisoners at Dumbarton castle. Confined in the Tower of London, they escaped by bribing the guards, to Germany, collected fresh forces from the con-federation, disembarked at Yarmouth, and marching to Verulam, were there routed and slain by the Pendragon. Uthyr Postumus, Pendragon, died at London, in his 90th year, A.D. 500. He was succeeded by his son Arthur, then in his twentieth year."

Piecing Together Arthur's Life

By contrasting the early historic references to Arthur with the earliest folk tales of him, we are able to have an idea of the sequence of events in his life.

The earliest historic references to Arthur refer to him as a soldier (Arthur miles') and as a battle leader (Dux Bellorum) and hint that his role was similar to that of his ancestors who operated from the Roman City of the Legion (York) and deployed their men along Hadrian's Wall and up to the Antonine Wall.

All 12 battles, described by Nennius, all have a northern feel to them and we can suggest that they represent Arthur, from around 490 to 510 defeating the Picts and Angles in northern campaigns.

We can then suggest a tactical retreat by Arthur, but one punctuated by his defeat of the Saxons at Badon. From 516 onwards his victory at Badon seems to have halted the advance of the enemy.

In Culhwch, Arthur suggests he is about 46 (two thirds of the way through his life, assuming he expected to live to 70) which would date the story at 516 - around the time of the Battle of Badon.

It has been suggested that the Arthur in Culhwch is one whose military victories, which brought him his status, are behind him and these are the days of a man whose legend is beginning to build.

Perhaps, after Badon, Arthur moved from his warlike northern Camelot (Camulod) to a more peaceful retreat in Gwynedd/Dyfed - as far away as possible from the Saxons.

We note in this period that the Arthurian tales begin to take on Irish characters - Arthur is given Caladwych (Excalibur), his mother's name is based on the Irish Grainne and his quests become more mythical, venturing to a western Otherworld.

It is fitting that Arthur's Cycle finishes as it begun with an historic military victory at Hadrian's Wall in 541 with the battle of Camlan.

166

Arthur began his career as a warlord, then the middle of his life was one of stories, songs, bards and tall tales, then it ended as it began, with a victory over the enemy.

On the Wikipedia page for King Arthur it currently says:

Historian Thomas Charles-Edwards doubted the existence of Arthur, saying "at this stage of the enquiry, one can only say that there may well have been an historical Arthur.... [but]....the historian can as yet say nothing of value about him".

Archaeologist Nowell Myres said: "no figure on the borderline of history and mythology has wasted more of the historian's time"

However we have proven a number of key events of an historical Arthur. Here I will leave aside things like his Round Table and famous sword, and concentrate on the facts:

1) Arthur is well documented in historic pedigrees, where he is listed as Arthwys ap Mor ap Ceneu ap Coel, the hereditary king of York who ruled circa 490-540.

2) Like his great grandfather Coel, Arthur held the title of Dux which meant he held command south of Hadrian's Wall. He was a descendant of Artorius Castus, after whom he was likely named. Both the title of Dux and the career of Artorius are well documented.

3) His main enemies were the Angles who invaded Northumbria. The rulers of Bernicia in Arthur's day were Esa, Eoppa and Ida. He fought them in several battles, notably including Glein, Dubglas, Guinnion and Badon in around 516.

4) Arthur fought his brother Morydd at Camboglanna near Hadrian's wall in around 537.

5) Arthur was alluded to by contemporary historian Gildas who called him The Bear (in Welsh Arth) and referred to as northern Welsh king as once having been his charioteer.

6) When Arthur died in around 540 his sons Keidyaw and Eleuther took power. Initially Keidyaw held Dumnonia and Dyfed with Eleuther taking York. Eleuther's son Peredur defeated Keidyaw's forces in 573 and took command of the three power bases.

7) After Arthur's death a number of kings named their sons in tribute to him including Meurig of Gwent, Peredur of Dyfed and Aedan of Dalriada.

8) Arthur's valour was recorded by bards Aneirin, Taliesin and Llywarch Hen in the 600s.

9) Arthur and his brothers Llaenauc, Einion, Cerdic and Morydd were fictionalised in early Welsh folklore like Culhwch and Olwen, Pa Gur and the Welsh Triads. They served as the basis for the characters Llew, Culhwch, Caradoc and Medraut. These tales probably date back to around 700.

10) Arthur's 12 battles were documented in the history of Nennius and the Annales Cambrae which date back to around 750.

There can now be no doubt that Arthwys ap Mar was the King Arthur of legend. He was born at precisely the right time. He lived from the late 5th century to the mid 6th century, and he was of course a King called Arthur.

But more than this, he was born into the dynasty of the Dux. The oldest reference to Arthur as a military leader calls him the Dux Bellorum, and this was the tradition Arthwys was born into. His great grandfather Coel was the Dux Brittania, his grandfather Ceneu the next Dux and his father and uncle likewise. Arthwys, like his great grandfather before him, defended the northern outpost of Britain. The "Old Renowned Boundary" as it was called by the bards.

Arthwys ap Mar, the Dux of Britain was the warleader who Nennius tells us defeated the enemy in 12 great battles. And the kings of Britain fought with him. He was the Bear who king Cuneglas followed, according to Gildas, and while King Arthur made Cai Hir his right hand man Arthwys ap Mar gave this honour to Cadwallon Lawhir. From Cadwallon Lawhir to Cai Hir to Sir Kay.

And King Arthur of course was the son of Uther, known in Gaelic as Iubher - the man of Ebrauc (York). And Arthur did defend the York area, much like Geoffrey of Monmouth tells us and his defence was the aptly named Camulod (Slack, West Yorkshire).

King Arthur was son of Uther son of Custennin, the real Arthwys was the son of "Iubher" (Mar) who was son of Ceneu. Custennin was a saintly king known as the blessed - as was Ceneu. In fact even Geoffrey of Monmouth recorded Ceneu as attending the coronation of Arthur.

Arthwys was also a close relative of the very men who recorded his exploits. He was a man of the north like the bards Aneirin, Taliesin, Myrdinn and Dunaut.

King Arthur had as his advisor the wise Merlin Emrys who as we know began his life as the boy Emrys who Vortigern tried to kill. In reality this Emrys (grandly called by Gildas "Ambrosius Aurelianus") was Pabo Post Prydain, the father and pillar of Britain and uncle of Arthwys. Pabo began as the military commander but then ended his life (at Llanbabo) as a monk. An old man by the time of Arthur's battles, Pabo was the basis for the court advisor Merlin who was also a combination of the later Myrdinn (who was the great grandson of Arthwys).

King Arthur's mother was the fair Igrainne son of "Amlawdd Gwledig". The real Arthwys was the son of Gwenllian whose father was a real Gwledig named Brychan ap Amlach. It is easy to see how Amlach Gwledig became Amlawdd Gwledig.

Then there are Arthur's brothers. In the earliest Arthurian stories, his companions included Llwch Llwch Llenlleawg (the prototype Sir Lancelot) and we aptly find Arthwys had a brother called Llenauc. Galahad was the son of Lancelot, Gwallawg was the son of Llenauc.

Lancelot's Joyous Garde in Benoic. The real Lancelot could be seen fighting at Bannockbur and his Joyous Garde was Din Guardi in Bamburgh.

Then there was Arthur's kinsman Einion (nicknamed Culwhch) so no surprise we find Arthwys had a brother called Einion. And of course Arthur's enemy was Mordred, usually a nephew, son or brother. Here we find Arthwys had a brother called Morhedd. Mordred's son was Mardoc, Morhedd's son was Madog.

The legendary King Arthur had a kinsman called Caradoc, Arthwys ap Mar had a brother called Ceredic. Arthur's sons included Gwydre, Arthwys had a grandson called Gwythre. But of course Arthur's court would be nothing without the ladies. King Arthur's wife was Gwenhwyfar who finished her days in a nunnery. Arthwys' wife was Cywair who finished her days as a saint.

Arthur had sisters called Morgan and Anna, Arthwys had aunts called Madrun and Anna. Arthur had Niniane or Nimue, Arthwys had Nyfainne.

When King Arthur died he passed his kingdom on to the son of Cador. When Arthwys died he was succeeded by his son Keidyaw. When he died Arthur passed his sword to Peredur, when the real Arthwys died his kingdom was claimed by his grandson Peredur.

It has been suggested King Arthur was descended from Lucius Artorius Castus, and Arthwys was descended from Lleifer Mawr ("Good King Lucius"). Lucius was said to be a Sarmatian, whose soldiers told a story of a sword being drawn from a stone.

The legendary Arthur fought at Camlann, Arthwys defended Hadrian's Wall at Camboglanna. After Camlann Arthur went to Avalon. Nearby to Camboglanna was Abvalanna. Arthur's sword was thrown to Vivianna the Lady of the Lake, the Hadrian's Wall garisson threw offerings to Coventina's Well. But Arthur's exploits were not restricted to the North, and neither were those of Arthwys. His son Keidyaw and grandson Peredur succeeded him in three kingdoms - Dyfed in the west, York in the North and Dumnonia in the South. These were the three courts of Arthur. In Dyfed he was the Protector Arthuir, remembered by the same Latin title as his great grandfather (Coel Hen Vortipor). In Dumnonia he was remembered as "Arthognou descendent of Coll" who built the sixth century garrison at Tintagel.

The more we look into Arthwys' genealogy the more we see the "knights" emerging. Cunomorus (King Mark) and Gorlois appear as Cinmarc ap Meirchionn and Gorlais. Gawain of Scotland emerges as Gabran of Dalriada. Ban and Bors were really Bran and Cincar. Uriens of course was Urien of Rheged, Tristan was Drustan the Pict.

The Arthur of legend fell at the hands of Eda. Arthwys was succeeded by Ida who conquered Bernicia when the Celts lost control of the north. Nennius is explicit in this. Immediately after telling us about Arthur, he tells us about the next ruler of north east England.

There is also ample evidence of the Arthwys dynasty reaching the continent. Pabo and Mar (Emrys and Uther) were recorded there as Pabo Riwal (Pabo the regal) and Reiuth (king Uther), naturally Arthur's fame spread there too.

Not only did he have garrisons in York, Dyfed, Cornwall and made excursions into Ireland and Scotland it is also likely he followed his father and uncle into Brittany.

A few years after his death, a Breton named Arthmael was born, and in Argyll, Aedan the son of Gabran (Gawain) called his second son Artur, a few decades later Peredur the grandson of Arthwys called his son Arthur as well.

The Aedd Mawr pedigree makes King Arthur the grandfather of Cadrod Calchfynedd via his son Amr Mawr (or Enir Fawr). In reality Arthwys was the great grandfather of Cadrod Calchfynedd via his son Cinbelin. In the original myths this son is recorded as Kynvelyn.

This pedigree leaves no doubt that Arthur and Arthwys were one and the same, sharing the ancestry of the famous Cadrod. In Arthwys we see every key element of Arthurian legend. We see the traditional Celtic warriors, the modern knights, the ladies, the saints, the battles, the swords and the holy springs. Arthur was not a composite of many Arthurs, he was simply King Arthur. However we will now look into the life of another king named Arthur who sheds further light on our quest - that was the later Arthur of Dyfed who I will call King Arthur II.

King Arthur II

We can define the extended Arthurian period as beginning with Magnus Maximus and his father in law Octavius (known respectively as Macsen and Evdaf). These two, ancestors of both the legendary King Arthur and the historic King Arthur, were also, in a way, prototypes for the Arthurian heroes, Romanised Britons, using the title of Gwledig - or Imperator. Of course we then come to the era of Constantine and the departure of the Romans, where again we find another who was ancestor to Arthur Pendragon and Arthwys of the Pennines - and that is Coel Hen.From Coel Hen we then meet the house of Vortigern and the house of Ambrosius, and Arthur's legendary father Uther.

Arthur, born in 470-475AD was born in the century when the Romans were still a recent memory. When he was a child names like Ambrosius, Riothamus and Agricola were associated with ruling Britain.

From being crowned in 485-490, fighting the Saxons, the Jutes, the Picts and the Irish, triumphing at Badon, he finally found himself in a new era. This was the era of civil war, where petty squabbles broke out from local tyrants like Maelgwyn, Morhedd, Cerdic and his own son.

Arthur fought at Camboglanna in about 540 and afterwards ended his days after abdicating his crown to his son Keidyaw. A generation later Keidyaw's son Gwendollau was fighting Peredur at Arthuret and Myrdinn the wizard disappeared into the forest.

With the death of Peredur in 580, the Arthurian age ended. Peredur, or Sir Perceval, was the last of the Knights of the Round Table. But he did leave one thing when he died. He left the name Arthur for his son.

Arthur of Dyfed (King Arthur II)
If Arthur ap Pedr did fight at Arthuret he would have been born no later than 560, making him 15 or so by the time of the battle. We do not know whether he was born in any of his father's three

main strongholds, York, Dyfed or Dumnonia but it would be a romantic notion to think he was born in Tintagel Castle.

In 580 Pedr is killed when Arthur II was about 20. Four years later the British were victorious over King Ceawlin of Wessex at the Battle of Fethanleigh.

In 613, when Arthur II was about 53, a united British force including warriors from Gwynedd, Powys, Pengwern and Dumnonia clashed with Aethelfrith's army at Chester. The leader of the British contingent is not named, but it would be nice to think it might have been Arthur II.

In 625 the Irish Annales record that Irishman Mongan was killed by "Arthur ap Bicuir" (probably Arthur ap Pedr). Arthur would have been 65 at the time, and probably drawing close to the end of his reign.

Arthur II may have begun his military career at Arthuret, he may have defended both Dumnonia and Dyfed. He may even have led the Britons against Ceawlin and Aethelfrith. He probably fought his last successful battle in Dyfed against Irish invaders. All in all, it seems Arthur II was a successful King but he did not, it seems, achieve a fraction of the accomplishments of his great grandfather King Arthur Pendragon.

Lineage:
Morgant m Eweint m Hoel m Rees m Arthuael m Ceingar merch Maredud m Teudos o Gantref Teudos. Teudos m Gwgawn m Cathen m Eleothen m Nennue m Arthur m Peder. Arthur m Peder m Kyngar m Gwrdeber m Erbin m Aircol Lawhir. Ayrcol lawhir m Tryphun m Ewein vreisc (m.) Cyndwr bendigeit m Ewein m Kyngar m Prwtech m Ewein m miser m Custennin m maxen wledic m Maximianus m Constantinus mawr m Custenint o Elen.

Alternative lineage of Dyfed:
    Constanti
    Constantini Magni
    Constans
    Pincr Misser
    Stater
    Eliud
    Ebiud
    Protector
    Protec
    Maxim Guletic
    Dimet
    Nimet
    Cloitguin
    Clotin
    Triphun
    Aircol
    Vortipor
    Congair
    Pedr
    Arthuir

As I have made clear, Arthwys of the Pennines was THE King Arthur of legend. I discount the claims that various unremarkable princes like Artur of Dalriada or Athrwys of Gwent contributed to his legend. However something about Arthur of Dyfed rings true as a King Arthur. That is why I call him Arthur II. For a start, he actually became king, unlike Artur and Athrwys (who pre-deceased their fathers).

Arthur of Dyfed was born about 20 years after Arthur of the Pennines died. He may have even been his great grandson.

If we accept that Peredur's father Eleuther was the son of Arthur, and confused with the other Eliffer, it would follow that Arthur, then Eleuther, then Peredur were the most dominant kings of York.

When Arthur II was born, his father ruled at the three main centres, York, Dumnonia and Dyfed. In York and Dumnonia he

174

is recorded as Peredur (later Sir Perceval) but in Irish Dyfed he was called Pedr, Retheior or Bicoir.

It is difficult to separate the exploits of the two King Arthurs, and so we can use only hypothesis. King Arthur I was the son of Mar of Ebrauc (Iubher or Uther) who was also called Riothamus King Arthur II was the grandson of Eleuther and son of Retheior - both shadows of the name Uther.

Arthur II may have fought, aged about 15, at the Battle of Arthuret. His father was victorious. Geoffrey of Monmouth's Vita Merlini places Myrdinn (Merlin) as an ally of Peredur (rather than the usual opposing side) so if this was the case, the ageing Merlin would have advised young Arthur.

Peredur was killed in about 580 when Arthur II was about 20. By this time his father had lost York and Dumnonia and so Arthur was only crowned King of Dyfed. Arthur II was contemporary with Owain ap Urien, Derfel Cadarn, Cadrod, Medraut II and a few other Arthurian characters.

Agricola in Dyfed is identical with Coel Hen (who lived to a very old age, hence the name) in York. Keidyaw in York is identical with Cincar in Dyfed and Cador in Dumnonia. Peredur in York is identical with Pedr in Dyfed and Peredur in Dumnonia.

We can see the following sequence of events:

1) Coel Vortepauc (Agricola Vortipor) is King in York and Dyfed
2) Ceneu became the next King in York
3) Ceneu was succeeded by his son Mar in York, while Erbin ruled Dumnonia and Dyfed
4) Arthur was Dux Bellorum and Vortipor
5) Arthur's son Cynvelyn became Vortipor (Dyfed)
6) Arthur's other son Keidyaw became king in York, Dyfed and Dumnonia
7) Arthur's grandson Peredur ap Eleuther became king in York, Dyfed and Dumnonia
8) Peredur was succeeded by Arthur II in Dyfed

Kings of Ebrauc, Elmet, the Pennines and Dux Bellorum	Kings of Dyfed	Kings of Dumnonia	Kings of Dalriada	Kings & princes of Ireland	Kings of Brittany	Campbell Ancestry	Legendary Kings
Coel Hen Guotepauc	Aircol lawhir (Agricola)					Coel	
Cunedda Gwledig							Vortigern
St Ceneu Guotepauc							St Constans
Pabo Post Prydain					Riwal		Ambrosius Aurelianus
Mar (Masguid Glof)	Etbin	Morvawr / Erbin	Fergus Mor	Muiredach	Riothamus	Muiris/Magoth	Uther Pendragon
Arthwys	Guortepir (Vortipor)	Gereint	Domangart	Mac Erca	Arthmael	Brearnaird	Arthur
Keidyaw	Congair	Cado / Constantine	Gabran	Constantine		Lidir	Constantine
Eleuther			Aedan				
Peredur	Retheior (Pedr)	Peredur				Iubbair	Peredur (Uther II)
Arthur	Arthur	Artuir	Artuir			Artuir	Arthur II

The real Cerdic

As Arthur is the greatest British (Celtic) hero and Cerdic is the forefather of the Wessex Saxons, surely they were enemies? Probably not. Actually they were brothers and allies.

Cerdic was the son of Elessa, father of Creoda and grandfather of Cynric.

Caradoc was the son of Llyr, father of Kowrda and grandfather of Kydeboc (according to the Hafod MS. 19(1536).

In the Bonedd y Saint, Kowrda becomes Cawrdaf, father of Medrawt. In another Bonedd, Kowrda is the ancestor of Kathan, the same as Cerdic's descendant Cutha.

In some legends of Caradoc, Vreichvras, the name of Llyr merini, is given as Eliavres - the same as Cerdic's father Elessa. Creoda is given Cynric as a son, Caradoc has Meuric. Llyr Marini (Llyr of the Sea) is the same as Mor (sea). Thus Cerdic is the ancestor of the kings of at least two kingdoms, Glamorgan and Wessex. Cerdic = Caradoc.

Acccording to Bartrum, the name Meuric was spelled in many different ways, including Mor and Amor. (Bartrum, 1966, p169, p205). We think that all of these are forms of the name which eventually became Henry in modern English, Henri in French, and Heinrich or Heimrich in German. Therefore, Arthwys ap Mor and Athrwys ap Meurig basically had fathers with the same name.

'Llyr' could arise from an elision of Eliavres. Furthermore, we are told that Eliavres, or Llyr merini, is a wizard. The words llyr and merini both have the same meaning in Welsh -'of the sea'. To have the two together seems redundant. However, in Old English it can make better sense. 'Lehr marini' would be 'master of the sea', 'teacher of the sea', or perhaps 'wizard of the sea'.

This may tell us something about Strongarm's father, and perhaps Strongarm as well. He must have been one the major shippers or merchants of the British and Gallic coasts. As such he would deal constantly with Saxons, both as crews and as piratical enemies.

While we're on the subject of the name of Strongarm's father, we have to mention that we still can't rule out Gorlois (Guor - Elessa) as being a form of this name. Recall that Geoffrey makes

Gorlois the occupant of a sea-protected stronghold and concocts a bizarre story in which Uther changes his image to that of Gorlois in order to seduce Gorlois' wife and conceive Arthur. Geoffrey could not have Arthur being the son of a wizard, so he created king Uther, a son of Constantine III, so that Arthur would be the rightful heir to the throne. Tatlock (1950, p313) is convinced that Gorlois, Igerna, and Uther are all inventions of Geoffrey of Monmouth, although we now suspect that the name Gorlois may have some basis after all. Arthur was son of Uther and Igraine (wife of Gorlois).

"How, then, may we account for the series of Wessex battles which span the period of supposed peace?" - Alcock (1971, p117)

There is no way Arthur and Cerdic could co-exist unless they were allies. The theory of Arthur and Cerdic being allies makes perfect sense. Let's look at the evidence:

Arthur's 12 battles named by Nennius took place in around 490-520. Most of these battles are clearly placed around Northumbria and between Hadrian's and Antonian Walls. For example Celidon (Caledonian), Tribruit (Edinburgh), Glein (Northmbria) and then there were the battles fought in Chester (City of the Legions), Durham (Guinnion Fort) and Wigan (Dubglas).

After Badon there was a generation of peace. This can be expressed as between 516, when Arthur won at Badon, and 547 when Ida took Bernicia. At the very same time that Arthur was defeating the Angles, Cerdic was ruling in the south. He was winning battles in Hampshire and Portsmouth and ruling all the way up until 534. So how could Arthur's reign have been one of victory if all the time Cerdic was winning? They were on the same side. Because they were brothers, sons of Mar.

Like their ancestors Coel Hen and Efdaf Hen respectively, Arthur and Cerdic were the Dux Bellorum and Dux Gewissae. Arthur was responsible for defending the north. Cerdic was responsible for defending the south coast. Cerdic succeeded

Vortigern the Elder as Dux Gewissae and Arthur succeeded Ceneu and Mar as Dux Bellorum.

Cerdic of Wessex is called in early sources "dux gewissorum", that is, "duke of the Gewissae". The British client-king, Octavius, who appears in ancient Welsh annals as Eudaf "Hen", who reigned in Britain during the Roman Era, was called "dux gewissorum" as an officer in Roman service before his usurpation of the British throne. And, the Dark Age "proud tyrant" Vortigern is referred to as "dux gewissorum" before he became King of Britain. Bede says that the West Saxons, who gave Wessex its name, were originally called "Gewissae" too.

Another clue to Cerdic's nationality is given by St. Gildas, who was a contemporary of Cerdic. He wrote in his "De Excidio" that the British victory at the Battle of Badon Hill [or Mount Badon], was so decisive that it gave the Britons a generation free from "barbarian" ["Saxon"] attacks, though the peace was often broken by the Britons fighting in civil wars among themselves.

The glaring contradiction between St. Gildas' assertion in his "De Excidio" that Britain was free of "barbarian" attacks for a generation - maybe St. Gildas did not consider Cerdic to have been a Saxon, but a Briton; nor the Wessex kingdom to have been a barbarian ["Saxon"] kingdom.

Arthwys and Cerdic were co-rulers of Britain - one was the Dux Bellorum, the other Dux Gewissorum. One made his base in York, the other in Wessex.

Vortigern revisited

The characters of Vortigern and Ambrosius – the two kings who ruled before Arthur or his father – are not usually disputed by historians. The sequence of events, however, seems to suggest a time period that would not allow Vortigern and Ambrosius to have been two people.

Some have suggested a hypothetical "Ambrosius the Elder" and "Ambrosius Aurelianus" versus "Vortigern the thin" and "Vortigern Vitalinus." I have suggested that the earlier Ambrosius was Amlach, and Ambrosius Aurelianus (Merlin Emrys) was Pabo Post Prydain. But what of Vortigern?

Genealogies would seem to suggest two men. In some records we see a "Vortigern the thin" – seemingly to distinguish himself from another Vortigern. We also see two wives, we have Vortigern marrying Severa, the daughter of Maximus, in about 425 (Vortigern would therefore have been born about 400). In about 455 we then have a Vortigern marrying Rowena, daughter of the Saxon Hengist. Vortigern is credited with sons named Catigern, Paschent and Vortimer, which parallels the later Dyfed chronology where Vortipor is succeeded by Congair and Pets.

If Vortigern Vorteneu, who married the daughter of Maximus, had a flourish of the mid 5th century, he corresponds perfectly with Ceneu ap Coel and Vorteneu with Ceneu.

If that were the case then Vortimer would be none other than Mar ap Ceneu. In the Cornish chronology he was called Mor-vawr (Mor Uther) here he is called Vorti-Mor. This would make Mor (Uther) the older brother of Pabo (Emrys) rather than younger as mythology has it, this fits in with what we know from Breton records and the story that Merlin outlived Uther. If Vortimer (Gwerthefyr) and Mor (Uthyr) were identical, this brings a fascinating new Arthurian dimension – since Vortimer was the father of Madrun and Anna, which is an obvious contrast with Uther, father of Morgan and Anna.

We again, have a new chronology, which rather than making things more complicated, actually simplifies matters:

Protectors of Britain after Rome

1) Coel Hen Vortepauc: Protector of Britain (Agricola)

2) Ceneu ap Coel Vortepauc (Vortigern Vorteneu)

3) Morvawr (Vortimer), Uther Pendragon (Mar)

4) Arthur (Arthwys)

5) Kynvelin, Keidyaw and Eleuther (sons of Arthur)

6) Peredur

7) Arthur II

In Arthur I we have the Arthur that Geoffrey of Monmouth wrote about. Arthur I was the King of Camelot and Caerleon, the husband of Gwenhwyfar, brother of Lugh, Culhwch and Mordred. He is the Arthur that Nennius described, the victor in 12 battles including Badon, who fell at Camlan.

Arthur I is the Dux Bellorum, the Great Bear of Britain and the Arthur celebrated by bards such as Aneirin and Llywarch Hen as Guletic and Emperor. He was the father of Anir, Llacheu, Gwydre and Cador and comrade of Kay and Bedevere.

Arthur II, born as heir to the kingdoms of Dyfed, York and Tintagel was the son of Uther II, kinsman to Gorlois. He was the father of Noe and killed a Mongan with a stone.

This finally solves the mystery of King Arthur's lineage. Since Geoffrey of Monmouth made Arthur the grandson of the emperor Constantine, British sources wanted to find Constantine in a genealogy. The only problem is, they chose the Constantine "son of Cador" who Arthur abdicated his throne to. They made his nephew into his grandfather. The real King Arthur I, son of Morvawr (Mor Uther) was succeeded by his sons Keidyaw (Cador), Eleuther (Llacheu or Uther II) and Kynvelyn (Amhar, Kynvor or Vortipor).

Keidyaw was succeeded in Dumnonia by Constantine, the man decried by Gildas. So now we meet Arthur II. His father Pedr (Peredur), once the Sir Perceval in Arthur I's Camelot is now another model for Uther, now referred to as Retheior, remeniscant of Uther I as Riothamus.

We have Arthur I, son of Morvawr of Iubher, who triumphed at Badon. And now we have Arthur II, son of Retheior ap Eleuther, king of Wales. Both were named Arthur and both were sons of "Uther".

In book one we identified that there were two Vortigerns and two Ambrosius. This is consistent with Arthurian research that typically refers to "Vortigern the Elder", "Ambrosius the Elder" and their younger counterparts. Vortigern the Elder was Vitalis, the Vortigern who married Severa, daughter of Magnus Maximus. He would have been born in around 400AD.

This Vortigern was also known as Vortigern the Very Thin (Gwrtheyrn Gwrtheneu). He was the son of Gwidol, probably a man of some importance from the Gloucester area.

Ambrosius the Elder was Amlach ap Tudwal, who fought Vortigern in 437AD at the battle of Wallop. Nennius records of the elder Vortigern: "During his rule in Britain he was under pressure, from fear of the Picts and the Irish ... and, not least, from dread of Ambrosius." Ambrosius was victorious and was "given all the kingdoms of the western side of Britain".

We then hear of another Vortigern. This time the man who bore the title was Ceneu, son of Coel Gautepauc (a British version of the title).

Ceneu was part of the confederation that invited the Saxons to Britain as mercenaries. Ceneu's sons were Pabo and Mar. Pabo went on to be known as Ambrosius Aurelianus (Ambrosius the Younger). There were clearly two Ambrosius. For Ambrosius to have challenged Vortigern in 437 he would have to have been born in around 400AD. Therefore he is unlikely to be the same man who was commanding 100 years later.

So the rulership was as follows:

Vortigern the Elder (Vortigern the very thin, Vitalinus)
Ambrosius the Elder (Amlach) - defeated Vortigern in 437
Vortigern the Younger (Ceneu) - invited the Saxons to Britain
Ambrosius the Younger and Uther (Pabo and Mar)
Arthur (Arthwys ap Mar)

One possibility is that Vortigern the Elder was to be identified with Cunedda. Vortigern was referred to as a man of Gwynedd, and that kingdom was founded by Cunedda. This gave us two lineages in Arthurian mythology, the lineage of rulership....
Vortigern, Ambrosius, Uther, Arthur.
And also the lineage of Arthur's ancestry....
Custennin (Ceneu), Uther, Arthur
But the confusion came when scholars saw Arthur II and mistook him for Arthur I.
This raises another tantalizing possibility. If Mar was Vortimer, that would mean he was the father of St Madrun and St Anna. In other words it means Uther Pendragon really was the father of Morgan and Anna!

Morgan: Daughter of Uther
Morgan Le Fay takes shape in the medieval romances of Chretien, but her origin is as a cross between the historic St Madrun and the Celtic Modron. Modron appears in Welsh Triad 70, in which her children by Urien, Owain and Morfydd, are called the "Three Blessed Womb-Burdens of the Island of Britain".
In about 1216 Gerald of Wales wrote that in the "fabulosi Britones" Morgan transported Arthur to Avalon to heal him. Morgan first appears by name in Geoffrey of Monmouth's Vita Merlini, written about 1150. Purportedly an account of the wizard Merlin's later adventures, it elaborates some episodes from Geoffrey's more famous earlier work, Historia Regum Britanniae.
In Historia, Geoffrey explains that, after Arthur is seriously wounded at the Battle of Camlann, he is taken off to Avalon, the Isle of Apples, to be healed.

In Chretien's Erec and Enid, completed around 1170; Morgan is mentioned when Arthur provides a wounded Erec with a healing balm made by his sister Morgan. Here she is a healer and provides the first mention of Morgan as Arthur's sister.

Morgan's role is greatly expanded in the 13th-century Vulgate Cycle. The youngest of Gorlois and Igraine's daughters, she is sent to a convent when Uther Pendragon kills her father and marries her mother. There she begins her study of magic.

The real life Morgan was St Madrun. The eldest daughter of King Vortimer (who we now know to be Mar). She was probably named after the Romano-British mother goddess, Matrona.

Madrun had married Prince Ynyr, a descendant of the Emperor Magnus Maximus, at a young age and, together, they ruled the Kingdom of Gwent. Could Ynyr have been Emrys (Merlin/Pabo) marrying his own young niece? This was not uncommon in those days.

On a pilgrimage to Ynys Enlli (Bardsey Island), Madrun and her handmaid, St. Annun, stopped for the night at Trawsfynydd. Here they both had an identical dream in which they were commanded to build a nunnery where they slept. Amazed by the coincidence, they did as required and the church there is dedicated to them still. She later settled in Cerniw with her son, St. Ceidio.

Anna appears in Arthurian mythology as both Anna and as Morgause. She is in Thomas Malory's 15th-century text Le Morte d'Arthur as the mother of Gawain and Mordred.In some later stories (such as the modern film Excalibur) her character is combined with that of Morgan.

The real life St. Anna of Oxenhall was the youngest daughter of Vortimer (Mar). She is supposed to have married Cynyr Ceinarfog (the Fair Bearded), Lord of Caer-Goch in Dyfed and the father of the legendary Sir Kay - but actually her husband was probably Prince Amon Ddu.

They had at least three children, Samson, Tydecho and Tegfedd. Amon became a monk at Ynys Byr (Caldey Island). Anna moved back to her native Gwent.

184

Vortimer

We know that in circa 530 the ruler of Dyfed was Voripor and we know that in circa 410 Coel Hen used the title Gautepauc, a British pronunciation of Vortipor.

We also have Vortigern the Elder, Vortigern the younger and "Vortimer" in the mid 400s. Therefore the title is a recurring one. I have theorised that Vortigern the Elder (Vitalinus) was succeeded by Ambrosius the Elder (Amlach) and that the identity of Vortigern the younger was Ceneu. He was therefore inheriting the mantle from his father Coel.

Next in line was Ceneu's son Mar who is both the Uther Pendragon and Vortimer of legend. We can see how Vortigern + Mor = Vortimor. But we can also see the similarities between the names Vortimer's Welsh translation Gwerthefyr and Uther.

It would also follow of course that Mor passed on the title to his son, King Arthur, which would explain why the ruler of Dyfed in Arthur's time was Vortipor (in Welsh Gwrthevyr) which again has resonance with the name Arthur, as in Gwrthevr-Arthwys.

The Dyfed lineage:

Erbin

Vortipor

Congair

Retheior

Arthur II

Arthurian lineage:

Morvawr (corresponds with Mor, Iubher, Uther, Erbin)

Kynvor (corresponds with Vortipor)

Constantine (corresponds with Congair)

Uther (corresponds with Retheior)

Arthur (corresponds with Arthur of Dyfed)

The Real House of Dumnonia

We have seen that the York Dynasty had rulership over the whole of Britain. Coel Hen was the Dux, he was followed by Ceneu, and he, by Mar and Pabo, and they by Arthur. Much like the Constantine, Uther, Emrys and Arthur of legend they were national overlords.

We know from the lineages of York, Dyfed and Cornwall, that Arthur was succeeded as national ruler by his son Keidyaw (Congair, Cador), and he by his nephew Peredur (Pedr, Pets, Retheior), and of course he by Arthur II. This raises an interesting possibility - that the kingship of Dumnonia never was.

The kingship of Dumnonia was supposed to include:
Erbin (circa 470)
Gereint (circa 500)
Cado and Cyngar (circa 540)
Peredur (circa 570)

Compare this with what we know of the Dyfed lineage:
Erbin (circa 470)
Gwrthefyr (circa 500)
Congair (circa 520)
Peredur (circa 570)

With what we have already identified:
Erbin = Mar = Vortimer = Uther Pendragon
Gereint = Gwrthefyr = Vortipor = Arthwys = King Arthur
Cado = Congair = Cyngar = Keidyaw = Cador
Peredur = Pedr = Pets = Retheior = Perceval

In the Welsh pedigrees, the one labelled X - Demetia gives a lineage of:

Erbin
Gereint
Cado
Pedur
Theudo [Tewdrig]
Peibiao
-
7 generations
-
Arthwael
Rees
hewel
Eweint
Morgan

Which all seems very typically Dumnonian - but then the lineage marked XI has:

Aircol [Agricola]
Erbin
Gordeber [Assumed to be Vortipor but could easily be Gereint - or both]
Kyngar
Peder
Arthur
-
8 generations
-
Arthwael
Rees
Hoel
Eweint
Morgant

What is clear is that not only was there clearly the same people on the throne of Demetia as Dumnonia - but there is also an obvious correlation with York.

Aircol is Coel, Erbin is Iubher, Gordeber is Arthwys, Kyngar is Keidyaw and then of course Arthur II is named after his famous ancestor.

In other words, Mar, Arthur and Keidyaw were national rulers. They were the Uther, Vortimer, Arthur, Cador and Constantine cited by Geoffrey. So why do we think that Erbin, Gereint and Constantine were kings of Dumnonia? Because they were actually kings of Damnonia by these names.

When Gildas tells us about Constantine, it is not clear whether he is referring to Cornwall or Scotland. He writes:

"This horrid abomination, Constantine, the tyrannical whelp of the unclean lioness of Damnonia, is not ignorant."

It is assumed Gildas means Dumnonia but is damning him in a pun, but this is not the case.

If we look again at the five kings Gildas talks about we have:

- Constantine (Constantine of Scotland)
- Vortipor (either Arthur himself, his son Kynvelyn)
- Aurelius Caninus (either Cynan of Powys or a son of Ambrosius)
- Maelgwyn (son of Cadwallon. Made claim to being Pendragon after Arthur)
- Cuneglasus (son of Owain. Former charioteer to Arthur's [the Bear's] stronghold)

Significantly though, we have seen that not only was King Arthur of the Ebrauc/Pennines dynasty but his greatness stretched from Scotland to Dyfed to Cornwall to Brittany. King Arthur was a Northern King by birth. But he was also king of Wales and Cornwall by his power.

The Coel-Vortigern-Mar-Vortimer-Arthur-Vortipor lineage confirmed

The "Life of St. Beuno" gives the following lineage:

Belim (Beli Mawr)
Amalech
Auallach
Eudoleu
Eudos
Elud
Eudegern
Eudegan
Deheuwynt
Rittegyrn
Gorthegyrnn
Gortheyrnn

Compare this to the lineage of Coel Hen given in the Harleian:

Beli
Aballac

Eudelen
Eudos
Ebiud

Outigern
Oudecant

Ritigirn

Iumetel
Grat
Urban
Telpuil
Teuhant
Tecmant

Coyl Hen Guotepauc

Here the earlier Gorthegyrnn is Coyl Hen Guotepauc and his son Gortheyrnn is Ceneu.

King Arthur II Timeline

Arthur II was born in around 565, some 105 years after his ancestor King Arthur. He was the son of Peredur, the Sir Perceval of legend who in Dyfed was recorded as Pedr or Retheior. Peredur was the son of Eleuther of the Great Retinue. So between his father having the name Retheior and his grandfather having the name Eleuther, we can see how some of his exploits could have caused him to be thought of as the son of Uther.

Arthur II may have been born in Dyfed or Dumnonia - his father ruled these places as well as York - but this Arthur seems more associated with Dyfed. His grandfather Eleuther was the kinsman of somebody called Gorlais so this could easily account for Geoffrey's story of Uther and Gorlois.

Arthur II's son Noe (Noah) was born in around 600 and Noe's son Cloten was born in around 630. Cloten married Ceindrych, unifying the kingdoms of Dyfed and Brycheiniog.

"The life of King Arthur : from ancient historians and authentic documents" by Joseph Ritson records a land grant by Noe ap Arthur II which states:

NOAH (Noe), the son of Arthur, fulfilling the commandment of the apostle, saying, " Give and it shall be given to you" and, elsewhere, ' as' is said, "The hand extending [itself] shall not be indigent," gave, for the commerce of the celestial kingdom, in the first time, the land Pennalun, with his territory, without any assessment to [any] earthly man, but only to god and the archbishop Dubricius and Landaff, founded in honour of Saint Peter

Arthur of Pennalun could perhaps be confused with the earlier Arthur Pendragon.

Arthur II alternative lineage in old Welsh texts tracing back to Constantine rather than Irish kings:
[O]uein map Elen merc Ioumarc map Himeyt map Tancoyslt merc Ouein map Margetiut map Teudos map Regin map Catgocaun map Cathen map Cloten map Nougoy map Arthur

map Petr map Cincar map Guortepir map Aircol map Triphun (map) Clotri map Gloitguin map Nimet map Dimet map Maxim gulecic (map) Protec (map) Protector (map) Ebiud map Eliud (map) Stater (map) Pincr misser map Constans map Constantini magni map Constantii et Helen Luicdauc que de Britannia exiuit ad crucem Christi querendam usque ad Ierusalem, et inde attulit secum usque ad Constantinopolin, et est ibi usque in hodiernum diem.

1) If Arthur II was the son of Peredur, he could have ruled from York to Cornwall, across to Dyfed.

2) If Noe was the son of Arthur II and was making land grants in Llandaff, then Arthur II ruled in Glamorgan as well

3) The Campbell genealogy suggests Arthur II ruled as far north as Scotland

4) If Arthur II (Arthur ap Pedr) is identical with Arthur ap Bicoir, then he could have also ventured to Ireland.

This Arthur appears in the 11th century Irish compilation The Annals of Tigernach. The annals gives a fragment of a poem by Bec Boirche, a 7th/8th century Ulster king and, presumably, bard.

Dyfed and Dalriada

In this study we have met a number of Kings and princes called Arthur. We have met Arthwys ap Mar (King Arthur I), Artuir ap Pedr (King Arthur II), Athwys ap Meurig (King Arthur III) and prince Artur Mac Aedan.

I have suggested that the Dyfed king list was not a pedigree and that Agricola, Vortipor, Congair, Pedr and Artuir were actually from the York dynasty - namely Coel, Arthur, Keidyaw, Peredur and Arthur II. But there are some strange possibilities with the throne of Dal Riada also.

Our King ARThur was the son of MOR. At the same time in Dalriada, DomangART was the son of Fergus MOR.

In the genealogies of the north we find a Garbaniaun who was son of Ceneu, son of Coel. Garbaniaun could be identical with Gabran.

Furthermore the Scottish Artur Mac Bicoir of Kintyre could be identical with Artuir ap Pedr of Pembroke. Kintyre, Pembroke and Tintagel all mean "headland". This could re-enforce the idea that both Arthur I and II were national rulers.

Bicoir is credited with killing the Irish king Mongan mac Fiachna Lurgan in 625. B- and P- are readily substituted for each other and -c- and -t- can easily be mistaken in manuscripts. In other words, it is possible that Artur mac Petuir and Arthur son of Bicoir, despite the slight chronological gap, are one and the same.

625 Mongan, son of Fiachna of Lurga was struck with a stone by Arthur son of Bicoir the Briton, and was crushed. About this, Bec Boirche said:

'Cold is the wind across Islay,
They shall commit a cruel deed in retribution,
They shall kill Mongan, son of Fiachna.
Where the Church of Cluan Airthir is today,
Renowned were the four there executed;
Cormac Caem, with screaming
And Illann, son of Fiachra;
And the other two, --

To whom many territories paid tribute,--
Mongan, son of Fiachna of Lurgan
and Ronan, son of Tuathal.'

Arthurian author August Hunt suggests Bicoir is a corruption of Petuir, as B and P can be interchanged. This would make it possible that Arthur ap Pedr and Arthur son of Bicoir, might be one and the same.

Arthur II Timeline

565 Arthur II, son of Pedr, is born, probably in Dyfed but possibly Tintagel.

570s The Northern British Alliance is forged between the kingdoms of Strathclyde, North Rheged, Ebrauc and Elmet. They fight the Northumbrians at the Battles of Gwen Ystrad and the Cells of Berwyn.

571 The Britons at Calchfynedd are defeated by King Cuthwulf of Wessex, at the Battle of Bedford.

573 Peredur and Gwrgi of Ebrauc, along with Kings Dunaut Bwr of the Northern Pennines and Riderch Hael of Strathclyde, marched north to claim the fort at Caer-Laverock from King Gwenddoleu of Caer-Wenddoleu.

573 Battle of Arthuret. Afterwards Myrdinn (Merlin II) goes mad and runs into the woods. It is possible Arthur II is present with Merlin.

580 Peredur (Perceval) is killed. He is succeeded by his son Arthur II, age 15.

590-610: The flourish of Arthur II as King of Dyfed

613 Arthur II, aged 48, is among Britons who defeat Aethelfrith's army at Chester

630s King Meurig of Glywysing and Gwent invades Ergyng

645 "The Hammering of Dyfed." Arthur II is presumably defeated by the Irish.

649 "Slaughter in Gwent"

665 The second Battle of Badon

Athrwys of Gwent (King Arthur III)

I disregard the hypothesis that Athrwys of Gwent could have been the real King Arthur - for a start he lived about 150 years too late. But he is still worth studying.

"Arthur was the British chieftain who so long resisted the progress of Cerdic. The unparalleled celebrity which this Briton has attained, in his own country and elsewhere, both in history and romance, might be allowed to exalt our estimation of the Saxon chief, who maintained his invasion, though an Arthur opposed him, if the British hero had not himself been unduly magnified into an incredible and inconsistent conqueror. The authentic actions of Arthur have been so disfigured by the additions of minstrels and of Jeffrey (Geoffrey of Monmouth) that many writers have denied that he ever lived: but this is an extreme, as objectionable as the romances which occasioned it. He was a chieftain in some part of Britain near its southern coasts. As a Mouric, king of Glamorganshire, had a son named Arthur at this period, and many of Arthur's actions are placed about that district, it has been thought probable that the celebrated Arthur was the son of Mouric: but this seems to have been too petty a personage, and too obscure for his greater namesake."

Sharon Turner - "History of the Anglo Saxons, Volume 1" (1805).

King Arthur Pendragon had been dead almost one hundred years and King Arthur II was probably coming to the end of his life.

A powerful ruler at this time was King Tewdrig of Dumnonia and Demetia, who may have been a nephew of Arthur II. In later life, he abdicated in favour of his son, Meurig, and became a hermit at Din-Teyryn (Tintern). Soon afterward, however, around 630, the Saxons invaded Gwent.

The local monasteries were particularly badly hit by their raids and so Tewdrig decided to come out of retirement and take up his sword once more to defend the church.

That year the West Saxons invaded Gwent But Meurig and Tewdrig defeated them at the Battle of Pont-y-Saeson. Tewdrig was wounded in the Battle of Pont-y-Saeson and had to be taken to Flat Holm in the Bristol Channel for treatment. An ox-cart was called to take him there but, on their journey, the oxen stopped themselves at a miraculous spring (now known as St.Tewdrig's Well). Here Tewdrig's wounds were cleansed and here he died. King Meurig built a great church on the spot and enshrined his father's saintly body there. The place became known Merthyr-Teyryn (Mathern) after the Martyred Prince.

In 635, King Meurig of Glywysing and Gwent invaded Ergyng and re-united the two kingdoms in the right of his wife. Meurig married Princess Onbrawst, daughter of King Gwrgan Fawr (the Great). Meurig's son was Arthwys or Arthur and he was born in around 620AD - he may have even been born one hundred years after Badon.

Arthur was the eldest son of King Meurig ap Tewdrig of Gwent & Glywysing. He and his father may have ruled jointly in the 640s and 50s, after Arthur became King of Ergyng in right of his mother. Upon the death of his maternal grandfather, King Gwrgan Fawr, in about AD 645, Arthur - presumably with the help of his father's armies - appears to have seized the throne of Erg-yng from his uncles, Caradog and Morgan. He may not have ruled the whole of Britain but we will still do him the honour of calling him King Arthur III.

The chronicles record that in 665 (when Arthur III was about 45) the Second Battle of Badon took place. Does this mean it was actually fought on the same battlefield as the first or does it mean that it was a sequel of sorts since the battle involved a King called Arthur defeating the Saxons? Since we have an Arthur III in Gwent, is it possible that the actual King Arthur I also ruled Gwent?

Arthur I in Gwent

As previously stated: Mor, Mouric, Meuric and Amor are variations of the same name. We know Arthwys ap Mor lived circa 470-540 and we know Athrwys ap Meurig flourished in the mid seventh century.

As we have demonstrated, Arthwys became a King, whereas Athrwys probably pre-deceased his father. Therefore is it possible that Arthwys ap Mor's kingdom extended to Gwent and that some of the records (such as those cited by Blackett and Wilson as proving Athrwys ap Meurig was the real King Arthur), could refer to Arthwys ap Mor?

For example - the Llandaff Charters name a King Arthwys ap Meurig as being contemporary with mid Sixth Century figures - perhaps it actually refers to the earlier man.

"Be it known to the clergy and people of southern Britain, that Athrwys, King of the Region of Gwent, granted to God and to St Duricius and St Teilo, and in the the hand of Bishop Comereg, the church of Cynfarch..."The king along carried the Gospel on his back and confirmed for ever the alms which had been given for the soul of his father Meurig..."

Another charter lists Coll (Coel?) and Morhedd (Morydd, Mordred) as well as Cynfyn (Cynvelyn?) which would again point towards Arthur I.

From History to Myth

So we have established the life of the historic King Arthur from 470 to about 540. Then we have seen another Arthur arise, the man's great grandson in around 555. Other kings were also inspired to name their sons Arthur, including Meurig of Gwent.

In the decades that followed, bards like Aneirin, Llywarch Hen and Taliesin recorded the exploits of Arthur in their war songs while historians like Gildas and Bede made records of the battles of the day.

When Gildas began writing in the 550s, Arthur was an old man dying. Gildas called him Vortipor. He also castigated Maelgwyn and three other kings among them Cuneglas who had been charioteer to the Bear.

By around 700AD chroniclers had a more complete picture of the life of Arthur. Nennius recorded his 12 battles against the Saxons and Scots/Picts. His most notable battle being Badon. The compiler of the Annales Cambrae recorded Badon and also the strife of Camlann where Arthur and Morydd (Mordred) fell.

Nennius and the Annales placed Arthur at precisely the right place in history – after Ambrosius and before Ida. Badon was placed accurately at 516, Camlann at 537 and Ida's rule at 547. Nennius also hinted that mythology had begun to come into play. He told an anecdote of Arthur battling his own son Amr (Cinbelin) and hunting for a great boar. Amr's grave had magical qualities and Arthur's dog left a magical footprint.

Despite being associated with myth and magic, Arthur was treated in a sober manner. He was Arthur Miles (Arthur the Soldier) and the Dux Bellorum (Duke of Battles). Similarly the bards paid tribute to his valour and leadership. The early Arthur had nothing to do with courtly love – he was a war leader.

In the years that followed, Arthur began to feature in Welsh folklore. In about 900AD Culhwch and Olwen was written. We know from the alternative version Einion and Olwen that Culhwch was also called Einion – and this was the name of one of the historic Arthur's brothers.

In Culhwch we see more references to the historic Arthur. His maternal grandfather was Amlawdd Gwledig – well known for fathering a number of saints. In reality this was Brychan ap Amlach. The name Amlach becoming Amlawdd which was more in vogue by the time it was written.

Arthur's allies Cadwallon Lawhir and Owain Ddantgwyn are integrated into the story as Cei and Bedwyr. Gabran makes an appearance as Gawain with the name Gwalchmai (possibly meaning Hawk of May). Arthur's brother Llaenauc appears, given some of the qualities of the Celtic god Lugh where he is called Llwch Llawwynniog. Even Gildas and Taliesin appear as warriors.

As well as Gwenhwyfar, tellingly a warrior is called Gwyn Hyfar. So perhaps somewhere along the way Cywair gained this name to become Guinevere.

The historic Arthur had a son named Cinbelin and he appears in Culhwch as Cydfan. Here he is the son of Arthur's mistress Eleirch – so maybe this is the reason he was discontent as an illegitimate son.

This Arthur is placed in Cornwall and, as we know, he held Tintagel there. Not only is Arthur descendant of Coel recorded on Tintagel's Arthur stone but his grandson Peredur is also well recorded as having inherited that land. The hunt for the boar takes place in Dyfed, the other land held by Arthur and Arthur II. Finally Arthur's advisor is Caradoc. This is another of Arthur's brothers Cerdic.

In Culhwch there are many mythical themes. One is Arthur's sword Caledvwlch, the later Excalibur.

In the Dream of Rhonabwy we meet more historic themes. Arthur's historic descendant Madog, son of Maredudd, is central and when he travels back in time we find Arthur and his northern kinsman Owain playing a board game.

While this symbolic game of cat and mouse takes place we learn that Arthur is about to fight Mordred at Camlann. The Arthur of Cullwhch and Rhonabwy is an older Arthur whose land is already gripped by civil war, not the young battle leader of Nennius.

Cerdic again features as Caradoc and Arthur's opponent at Badon is revealed as Osla Big Knife. Arthur's cousin Cinmarc appears as March, son of Meirchionn but here he is ruler of the Norwegians!

Badon is identified as Buxton, but we will also consider Caer Faddon. As Ashley points out that whether or not Faddon was Badon is beside the point - at this point the Britons probably believed Faddon to be Badon and this is likely where the legend developed from.

In the poem Pa Gur we learn more about the mythology of Arthur, but again based on the historic Arthwys ap Mar. His father Mar, king of Ebrauc appears as Uther and again we meet Bedwyr and Cei. Llaenauc makes another appearance as Llwych of the Striking Hand. We also meet Arthur's other son Llacheu who I have identified with Eleuther son of Arthwys.

Next we look to the Welsh Triads. Here Arthur is given three courts – one in the north, one in Cornwall and one in Wales - and we know this was the case. Again Medrawt is identified as the villain. Arthur's uncle Pabo Post Prydain and Llaenauc son's Gwallawg along with Cynfelyn are named as Pillars of Battle and three more northern rulers Cynfawr, Gwenddoleu and Urien are named as Bull Protectors of Britain.

How the Arthur of early mythology became the medieval king of Mallory is not straightforward. It is clear to see that Cei became Sir Kay, Bewyr became Sir Bedevere, and it can be argued that Llwch became Lancelot and Gwalchmai became Gawain.

Elements of Geoffrey of Monmouth are clearly taken from older sources: But as we read works like Geoffrey of Monmouth it is clear another event has worked its way into Arthur's story - and that is Arthur's world domination!

In Geoffrey, not only does Arthur unite Britain he also conquers France, Normandy, Skandinavia and while he's at it conquers the Roman Empire!

Arthur goes from a great British warleader to a world beating emperor. Two theories have been offered for this:

a) Geoffrey wanted Arthur to be on a par with other national heroes like Charlemagne and Alexander the Great so he exaggerated the extent of his rule.

b) Geoffrey confused Arthur with somebody who actually did conquer places like Rome and Greece. Blackett and Wilson have suggested that Magnus Maximus (pretender to the emperorship of Rome) had a son called Arthun (actually he was probably called Andragathius and probably wasn't Maximus' son) who was known as "king of Greece" and subdued Rome, since he captured and murdered the Roman Emperor Gratian in 383.

I however propose another theory. Geoffrey simply took a throw-away comment in Culhwch and Olwen and took it literally. Culhwch and Olwen was an exercise in typical celtic "blarney". Everything in it is exaggerated for excitement or to make rhymes. Everyone in the story has a fantastic quality, they are the biggest, the strongest, the handsomest, the ugliest, they can slay giant pigs and ride on the back of salmon.

At one point Arthur wheels out his own credentials. He is full of celtic "blarney" and exaggeration, saying: "I have been heretofore in India the Great and India the Lesser; and I was in the battle of Dau Ynyr, when the twelve hostages were brought from Llychlyn. And I have also been in Europe, and in Africa, and in the islands of Corsica, and in Caer Brythwch, and Brythach, and Verthach; and I was present when formerly thou didst slay the family of Clis the son of Merin, and when thou didst slay Mil Du the son of Ducum, and when thou didst conquer Greece in the East. And I have been in Caer Oeth and An- noeth, and in Caer Nevenhyr; nine supreme sovereigns, handsome men, saw we there, but never did I behold a man of equal dignity with him who is now at the door of the portal."

All that happened is that Geoffrey understood that many of Arthur's exploits (such as Badon and Camlann) were historical events, and so he assumed that the exploits in Culhwch must have had an historical basis too, and so Geoffrey weaved in Arthur's world domination along with his domestic battles.

Arthur's battles against the Saxons are found in the 9th-century Historia Brittonum by Nennius. These battles were also described by Gildas. The battle of Camlann is taken from the Annales Cambriae.

Arthur's personal status as the king of all Britain is found in Culhwch and Olwen, and in Nennius he was Dux Bellorum. The five kings who ruled after Arthur or towards the end of his life are taken from Gildas.

Sir Kay comes from the earlier "Cai Hir"; Sir Bedivere is derived from "Bedwyr" and Sir Gawain is "Gwalchmai" in Welsh. Geoffrey's Guanhumara is based on Gwenhwyfar, his Uther is based on Uthyr and his Caliburnus on the sword Caledfwlch. Mordredus is taken from Medraut. Even Arthur's conquering of Europe and Africa are taken from a throw-away line in Culhwch.

In Book 2 we have investigated the hypothesis that not only was Arthwys the warleader of Badon who defeated the Angles in 12 battles ruling from York, but he was also a national Dux who defended the four corners of Britain.

Nennius tells us of a young Arthur, a warleader defending the Northern and Eastern frontiers, but the early folklore places him in Cornwall (the Southern Frontier) and Dyfed (the Western Frontier) as a much older man.

The genealogies suggest this was very much the case. In the pedigrees of York, we see Arthur succeeded by Eleuther, Keidyaw and Cinbelin and subsequently Eleuther by Peredur, Keidyaw by Gwendollau and Cinbelin by Cadrod Calchfynedd. But in the pedigrees of Dumnonia we see that after the time Arthur would have ruled, he was succeeded again by Keidyaw and he by Peredur. And in the pedigrees of Dyfed, Vortipor (whether he was Arthur or a contemporary of Arther) was succeeded by Keidyaw and he by Peredur. And so we seem to have the situation where Arthur handed over his kingdom to his son Keidyaw, but then Keidyaw lost Dumnonia and Dyfed to his nephew Peredur.

This situation is not speculation - it is recorded fact, because we know that Peredur's army met Keidyaw's army (led by his son

Gwendollau) at Arthuret in 573AD, where Peredur was victorious and so captured the entire kingdom of Britain.

As if to solidify his dynasty as the rightful rulers of Britain, Peredur named his son Arthur. This Arthur II would inherit the kingdoms of Ebrauc, Demetia and Dumnonia. Like his great grandfather Arthur, this Arthur II was overlord of Britain. Is Arthwys remembered in Ireland?

In Book 1 is discussed Arthwys and Llaenauc's excursion to Ireland (as told in Culhwch etc) and his Irish wife Cywair (Gwenhwyfar).

In Book 2 I demonstrated that names like Keidyaw and Peredur were at the same time in the pedigrees of Arthur's 'three kingdoms', York, Dyfed and Tintagel.

Now we have seen that in the pedigree of Dalriada, names from the Coel dynasty like Garbaniaun, Mor and Arthur appear in the pedigree of Dalriada as Gabran, Fergus Mor and Domangart. But could Arthur's presence also be felt in Ireland? So in around 490AD, the ruler in York was Mor, the ruler in Dumnonia was Morvawr, the ruler in Dalriada was Fergus Mor. One generation later we see Arthur, Arthwys or Domangart.

Strangely enough in the same generation as Mar (Mor, Morvawr, Fergus Mor) we find Muiredach. Muiredach's son was Mac Erca, a strange name explained that his mother was Erc a British princess. But men did not take their mother's names as surnames. Why was he not called Mac Muiredach?

Where did Mac Erca come from? Dane Pestano suggests that Mac Erca was none other than King Arthur and that Mac Erca comes from Arthur's title Mab Uter - in turn Mab Ursa. In Welsh bear is Arth, in Latin bear is Ursa.

Arthur was called Arthur Mab Uter in one record (translated as Arthur, terrible son or take to be confused with Arthur ap Uther) - regardless he could easily have been called Arthur Mab Ursa, which was recorded in Ireland as Arthur Mab Erca. If King Arthur the Bear really is remembered in Ireland as Mab Ursa or Mac Erca then it is very telling that his father is Muiredach - or Mor.

At the same time is another Muircertach Mac Muiredach and her it seems we have Arthwys' brother Cerdic ap Mor (Certach Mac Muire). The timeframe for Mac Erca fit perfectly for Arthur as well. Mac Erca is recorded as dying in about 534AD, Arthur in around 539AD.

Could Mor, Muiredach and Fergus Mor all be the 'English', Irish and Scots names for the same man? - Uther Pendragon.

Could Arthwys, Mac Erca and Domangart all be the 'English', Irish and Scots names for the same man? - Arthur Pendragon.

Mac Erca also had a supernatural death. He was also the father of Baetan, identified by some as related linguistically to the Battle of Badon. Mac Erca also had a son named Constantine - while the legendary Arthur was succeeded by Constantine son of Cador and Arthwys' son was Keidyaw.

In the Irish version of the Historia, it is stated: "and Mac Erca then committed an additional sin, that is, he took to himself the wife of Luirig, after many battles and conflicts with the king of France, to take his daughter from him, until at last the daughter fell into Mac Erca's hands, and she bare him four sons, viz. Constantine, and Gaedhal-Ficht (from whom descend the kings of Britain, and the kings of Britain-Cornn); Nellenn (a quo gens Nellan), and Scannal..."

The names of Coel, Ceneu, Mar, Pabo, Arthwys, Keidyaw and Peredur are listed in York. These correspond to Agricola, Vortipor, Congair and Pedr in Dyfed. These in turn correspond to Erbin, Constantine and Peredur in Dumnonia. These may also correspond to Fergus Mor and Domangart in Scotland. And to Muiredach, Mac Erca and Constantine in Ireland. And to Riothamus and Pabo in Brittany.

If this hypothesis is correct then Arthwys as Dux Bellorum was influential not only in his native York and the Pennines but all four corners of the British Isles and Brittany.

The Lost Book of King Arthur

Pa gur, is an incomplete Middle Welsh Arthurian poem in the Black Book of Carmarthen. It presents a dialogue between Arthur and Glewlwyd the gate-keeper, followed by a lengthy monologue in which Arthur boasts of his splendid retinue of heroes, above all Kei, in order that they may gain access to some unspecified hall.

In this way, the poem takes pride of place as one of the earliest pieces of literature to offer a catalogue of Arthur's retinue, with incidental allusions to miscellaneous Welsh legends, a number of which are associated with Arthur himself.

The basic structure of one or several heroes seeking admittance to a hall through a series of boasts extolling his/their deeds and qualities has parallels elsewhere in early Welsh and Irish literature.

The poem opens with Arthur and his companion Kei asking about the identity of the gate-keeper (porthawr), who reveals that his name is Glewlwyd Gafaelfawr ("Mighty-Grasp").

When Arthur declares that he has the best of heroes with him, Glewlwyd does not allow them inside unless their worth has been established one way or another.

This brief conversation is the starting point for a monologue uttered by Arthur, which takes up the greater part of the poem. We should note that Glwelwyd becomes Arthur's porter in Culhwch and Olwen and The Dream of Rhonabwy.

Pa Gur mentions Uther Pendragon: "Mabon, the son of Modron, The servant of Uthyr Pendragon."

The Battle of Tribruit is mentioned: "Did not Manawyd bring perforated shields from Trywruid? And Mabon, the son of Mellt, Spotted the grass with blood?"

Llwch is identified as a guardian of Hadrian Wall based around Edinburgh, supporting his identification with Llanauc: "And Llwch Llawynnog - Guardians were they On Eiddyn Cymminog, A chieftain that patronised them."

Kay was also fighting in Edinburgh: "Cai, as long as he hewed down. Arthur distributed gifts, The blood trickled down. In the hail of Awarnach, Fighting with a hag, He cleft the head of Paiach. In the fastnesses of Dissethach, In Mynyd Eiddyn."

Cynvyn is mentioned. Is this Arthur's son Cynvelyn? "He contended with Cynvyn."

Bedevere is also mentioned, again fighting at Tribruit: "By the hundred there they fell, There they fell by the hundred, Before the accomplished Bedwyr. On the strands of Trywruid, Contending with Garwlwyd."

Bedevere and Kay are identified as commanders of 900 men, defeating 600, comparable to Nennius's record of Arthur killing 900: "Brave was his disposition, With sword and shield; Vanity were the foremost men Compared with Cai in the battle. The sword in the battle

Was unerring in his hand. They were stanch commanders of a legion for the benefit of the country- Bedwyr and Bridlaw; Nine hundred would to them listen; Six hundred gasping for breath Would be the cost of attacking them."

Emrys also seems to be mentioned: "Servants I have had, Better it was when they were. Before the chiefs of Emrais."

The poem records the deaths of Cai and Llacheu, who we have identified with Cadwallon and Eleuther.

"There was no day that would satisfy him. Unmerited was the death of Cai. Cai the fair, and Llachau, Battles did they sustain, Before the pang of blue shafts. In the heights of Ystavingon Cai pierced nine witches. Cai the fair went to Mona, To devastate Llewon. His shield was ready Against Oath Palug When the people welcomed him. Who pierced the Cath Palug? Nine score before dawn

Would fall for its food. Nine score chieftains..."

Conclusion

The original King Arthur was Arthwys ap Mar. Born in around 470AD, he defeated the Angles and Saxons in 12 battles in the early 500s culminating with the Battle of Badon in 516AD. His parents were Mar of Iubher and Gwenllian.

His uncle Pabo was known as the Father and Pillar of Britain and he succeeded his grandfather Ceneu and great grandfather Coel as Dux Bellorum.

To Northern British scribes, Arthwys became Arthur, Iubher became Uthyr and Ceneu became Custennin.

Coel was known as Agricola the Protector (Vortepauc) and his son Ceneu inheritted the title (Vortigern), he foolishly invited the Saxons to Britain, something his sons would pay for. Mar assumed the title Vortimor (Vortimer). After Arthur's triumph at Badon he assumed the title protector (Vortipor).

To Demetian scribes, they were known as Vortigern and Vortimer; and Agricola and Vortipor.

Over the next few decades tales were told of Arthur, his brothers and their wives. Einion won Olwen, Llaenauc helped Arthur invade Ireland and Llwch Llaeminauc became known as his greatest warrior.

Many years later, Llaenauc and his son Gwallawg became Lancelot and Galahad, just as Arthur's wife St Cywair became Gwenhwyfar.

Arthur's other brothers Morydd and Cerdic (In Wales Medraut and Ceretic) became Mordred and Caradoc. Arthur led kings like Cadwallon Law Hir into battle. He became Cadwallon Hir, then Cado Hir then Cai Hir and finally Sir Kay.

Arthur's sons were Keidyaw, Kynvelyn, Eleuther and Greidol. In later legends they were known as Cador, Amhar, Llacheu and Gwydre.

Arthur died after Camlann (Camboglanna on Hadrian's Wall) and afterwards his family fought for succession of the British throne. Men like Peredur (later Sir Pereval), Myrdinn (Merlin) and Keidyaw battled for the crown.

In the end, Peredur succeeded Keidyaw. In Dyfed they were recorded as Pedr and Congair or Retheior and Cincar. Peredur's successor to the three kingdoms of York, Dyfed and Cornwall was Arthur II (Arthur ap Pets) who was born in around 565AD, some 90 years after Arthur I (Arthwys ap Mar). However, now came errors transcribing the lineages. Vortipor (Arthur), Congair and Pets were shifted back in time - Vortipor became confused with Vortimer and Congair and Pets became Catigern and Pascent.

Chroniclers always knew that Arthur was the son of Iubher (Mar) son of Custennin (Ceneu) but in trying to complete the lineage they muddled him up with Arthur II. After all, he too succeeded two men with names very similar to Iubher/Uther - namely Retheior and Eleuther. And he in turn succeeded someone with a very similar name to Constantine - Congair.

And so the lineage should have been:
Arthur - Iubher - Ceneu - Coel Vortepauc.

But this got mixed up with:
Arthur II - Eleuther - Congair - Vortipor (Arthur I) - Mor-Iubher - Ceneu – Coel.

And the resulting lineage was drawn up as:
Arthur - Uther - Custennin - Kynvor - Morvawr - Cadfan – Cynan.

In Wales therefore the Arthurian lineage seen in the Harleian and Bonedd pedigrees is a combination of both Arthur I and Arthur II.

However Geoffrey of Monmouth's British source used the original lineage and cited and albeit jumbled arrangement of the correct people. He originally calls Arthwys "Artgualchar of Warwick" son of Morvidus (whose brother is Gorbonianus) and his brother is Elidurus. Here Geoffrey takes Arthwys, Mar, Eleuther and also Peredur and pushes them centuries back. He does however leave Ceneu and Pabo as guests at Arthur's coronation and most of Uther's fighting is done in and around York.

The Arthur I and Arthur II hypothesis proven in Scotland

In Scotland, the lineages of clan Campbell and MacArthur maintain the Coel-Ceneu-Iubher-Arthwys genealogy and the Enir Fardd lineage confirms that Cadrod Calchfynedd's grandfather Cynbelin was none other than Amhar.

One Scottish pedigree gives Artuir mic Iubair mic Lidir mic Brearnaird mic Muiris mic Magoth mic Coiel. This would appear to marry up somewhat with Arthur son of Uther son of Eleuther son of Arthur son of Mar [son of Masguid] son of Coel. Here it seems to the Scots genealogists 'the' King Arthur was actually Arthur II of Dyfed.

A full pedigree states: Dubhghaill Caimbel a quo [Muintir Chaimbeil] m. Eoghain m. Donnchaidh m. Gille Choluim m. Duibhne (o raitear Meg Dhuibhne) m. Feradaigh m. Smerbe m. Artuir m. Iobhair m. Lidir m. Bernaird m. Muiris m. Magoth m. Coill m. Cotogain m. Caidimoir m. Catogain m. Bende m. Mebrec m. Grifin m. Briotain.... or Arthur m. Ybar m. [E]lidir m. Bernard m. Meuris m. Magodd m. Coel m. Cadwgan m. Caid mawr m. Cadwgan m. Bende m. Mebrig m. Gryffyn m. Prydain

One theory is that Smervie, the fool of the Forest, is actually Myrdinn which would be about the right generation and explain the madness in the forest and the Scottish connection.

Campbell, in his "West Highland Tales," gives a "Genealogy Abridgment of the very ancient and noble family of Argyle, 1779."

The writer says this family began with Constantine, grandfather to King Arthur; and he informs us that Sir Moroie Mor, a son of King Arthur, of whom great and strange things are told in the Irish Traditions - was born at Dumbarton Castle, and was usually known as "The Fool of the Forest"

Therefore, in conclusion, the only man who was ever The King Arthur was Arthwys ap Mar (475-540). His lineage became somewhat muddled with his own great grandson Arthur ap Pedr over time, but that does not change the life of the man who ruled from Hadrian's Wall down to Tintagel.

Arthwys ap Mar ap Ceneu (King Arthur son of Uther son of Custennin) was the Dux Bellorum from Hadrian's Wall to York to Dyfed to Tintagel. He defeated the Saxons in 12 battles. His commanders and allies were Llaenauc and Gwallawg (Lancelot and Galahad), Cadwallon and Owain (Kay and Bedevere), Gabran (Gawain) and his son Keidyaw.

He was advised by the hermit Pabo (Merlin Emrys) and his wife was Cywair (Gwenhwyfar). He was descended from Lucius Artorius Castus (Lleifer Mawr) and Octavius (Evdaf Hen). He was betrayed by Morydd (Mordred) and Cynvelyn (Amhar).

After his death Myrdinn (Merlin II), Peredur (Perceval) and other rulers contested his throne.

Arthur II, son of Retheior ap Eleuther (Uther II), succeeded as King from York to Dyfed and Tintagel.

Arthur was the once and future king.

Pedigree of the Clan Campbell	Descent of the Kings of Dyfed/York
Coiel	Coel Hen (Agricola)
Magoth	Ceneu
Muiris	Mar
Breamaird	Arthwys
Lidir	Eleuther
Iubhair	Retheior/Peredur
Artuir	Arthur II

Timeline

306AD Emperor Constantius dies in York

306AD Constantine I, born in York becomes Emperor of Rome

335AD Magnus Maximus (Macsen Gwledig) is born

Circa 300AD Coel Hen is born in the north, probably near York

383AD Magnus Maximus declares himself Emperor in Britain

388AD Magnus Maximus dies

Circa 400AD Coel's future son in law Cunedda (later Vortigern The Elder) and Ceneu (later Vortigern Vortineu) are born

400s Amlach (Ambrosius the Elder) is born to Tudwal and Gratiana (daughter of Magnus Maximus)

410AD British emperor Constantine III withdraws his men from Britain

410AD Northern British Chieftain Coel Hen (Agricola) is elected Protector of Britain (Vortepauc). His headquarters is York and his legion patrols Hadrian's Wall as Dux Bellorum

420AD Coel Hen dies. Northern Britain is divided between Ceneu and Germanus. Ceneu (Constantius) succeeds his father Coel as Protector

c.425 Cunedda Wledig and his retinue are moved south from Manau Gododdin to Gwynedd in order to expel the invading Irish.

420s Vortigern (Cunedda) marries Magnus Maximus' daughter Severa

425AD Vortigern comes to power in Southern Britain

428AD Vortigern invites Saxons Hengist and Horssa to Britain

c.430 Death of Tewdrig of Garth Madrun. His son-in-law, Prince Anlach, inherits.

c.437 Amlach marries Ribwast, daughter of Vortigern. War breaks out between the Irish settlers in Garth Madrun and Powys. King Anlach of Garth Madrun is defeated and forced to send his son, Brychan, as a hostage to the Powysian Court.

437AD Vortigern fights Ambrosius the Elder (Amlach Gwledig) at Wallop

450AD Ceneu's son Emrys is born. His Roman title is Ambrosius Aurelianus. He will later be known as Pabo Post Prydain – the Father and Pillar of Britain

450AD Ceneu's son Masguid is born. He will also be known as Morvawr (Mor Iubher) or simply Mor or Iubher (Uther).

450AD Ceneu "inflicted a massacre" on the enemies of Britain, the Picts and Irish, and they are left in peace for a brief time.

467AD Vortigern (Cunedda) is burnt to death while being besieged by Ambrosius Aurelianus at Ganarew.

470AD Ambrosius is crowned king of the Pennines (Pabo Post Prydain)

Masguid is crowned king of York (Iubher) and Westmorland

470AD Ambrosius (Pabo) succeeds as ruler in Britanny. He is known as Pabo Riwal Mawr Marchou. In Britain he establishes a unit called the Ambrosiaci. These garrisons surrounded the old territory of the Dobunni which was known as Calchvynedd (Cotswolds).

In Britanny his brother Mor (of Armorica) becomes known as Ur-Ben (a contraction of Uther Pen) or Erbin.

470AD Masguid (Mor) and Gwenllian (Igraine) have their first son Arthwys (Arthur). He is followed by Llaenauc (Lancelot), Moryedd (Mordred), Cerdic (Carados) and Einion (Cullhwch)

475 AD Arthur's uncle Emrys (Pabo Post Prydain) takes him to Dyfed where he is looked after in the court of Einion Yrth (Ector) and grows up with Einion's sons Cadwallon (Cay) and Owain (Bedevere).

477AD Saxon leader Ælle proclaims himself Bretwalda (king of Britain) in Sussex

484AD Ambrosius Aurelianus fights Ælle's Saxons before finally abdicating in favour of his nephew Arthur

485AD Arthwys ap Mar is crowned King of Northern Britain, ruling from Camulod at what is now Slack in Yorkshire.

488AD Ælle, the Bretwalda in Sussex also proclaims himself king in Cantwarra.

490-510 Arthur defeats the Bernicians at the battle of Glein in Northumberland.

Arthur and Llaenauc defeat the Saxons in four battles along the River Douglas

Arthur defeats Pictish rival Caw at the Battle of Bassas. Caw is the father of Gildas.

Arthur wins a battle in the Caledonian forest.

Arthur defeats the Saxons at Vinovium Fort in Durham

Arthur defends York (City of the Legions) against the Saxons and is proclaimed Dux Bellorum – Leader of Battles.

490s Arthwys, Llaenauc and Einion embark on a quest to Ireland where Arthur meets his Guinevere – Cywair of Ireland, and gets his fabled sword.

Arthur and Cywair's sons are born. They are Keidyaw (Cador), Cinbelin (Amhar), Eleuther (Llacheu) and Greidal (Gwydre). Llaenauc (Lancelot) has a son named Gwallawg (Galahad)

495 Arthur's brother Cerdic becomes count of the Saxon Shore (Dux Gewissae)

501 Cerdic makes Port, Bieda and Maegla his mercenary commanders

508 Cerdic defeats Natanleod

Arthur defeats his enemies at the battle of Tribruit

Arthur defeats his enemies in Agned (Edinburgh).

After 11 decisive victories he holds Northern Britain safely. He also rules from Demetia (Dyfed) in the West and Tintagel in the South

514 Cerdic invites more mercenaries to Britain and wins another battle

516 Arthur defeats the Saxons at the Battle of Badon. Cerdic proclaims himself king in Wessex

Arthur's rebellious son Cinbelin proclaims himself with his great uncle's titles "Pabo Post Prydain" father and pillar of Britain in Calchfynedd and is known as Amhar Mawr (Ambrosius the great)

520s Arthur reigns Britain and Britanny as Pendragon, Dux Bellorum, Gwledig and Imperator Emperor

530 Cerdic conquers the Isle of Wight

530 Saint Pabo Post Prydain (Merlin Emrys) dies at Llanbabo.

537 Arthur fights his brother Morydd (Mordred) at the Battle of Camlann (Camboglanna in Northumberland).

Arthur is gravely wounded and Morydd is killed.

540s Probable writing of Gildas' "De Excidio Britanniae." He doesn't mention Arthur but refers to the Bear's Stronghold (Bear in Welsh is Arth)

540s Arthur abdicates his throne to his eldest son Keidyaw who makes Cadbury his southern base

550 Cinbelin's son Cynwyd marries Greidol's daughter Peren uniting the 'Amhar' and 'Gwydre' lines. Their son is Cadrod

558 Death of Gabran (Gawain)

565 Arthur's grandson (from his son Eleuther-Llacheu) Peredur calls his son Arthur II. Artuir Mac Aedan Mac Gabran is also born

570 Death of Gildas

570s Northern British Alliance under Arthur's grandson Peredur

571 Cuthwulf of Wessex defeats Cadrod of Calchfynedd

573 The battle of Arthuret. King Arthur's grandsons Peredur and Gwrgi fight Arthur's other grandson Gwenddoleu. His bard Myrddin (Merlin) is present.

580 Peredur of York, Dyfed and Dumnonia is killed. His son Arthur II succeeds him

C600 Aneirin writes the Gododdin and mentions King Arthur I

613 Aethelfrith defeats Arthur II at Chester

620 Athrwys ap Meurig is born

645 The Hammering of Dyfed. Defeat of Arthur II

665 The second battle of Badon. Athryws (Arthur III) possibly involved

830 Nennius writes Historia Brittonum, listing Arthur I's battles

50 Arthurian Characters Identified in History

1) **Agravain/Rhufon:** Rhun ap Maegwyn
2) **Amhar:** Cynvelyn ap Arthwys
3) **Amlawdd Gwledig:** Brychan ap Amlach Gwledig
4) **Anna:** St Anna
5) **Artegall:** Arthwys ap Mar
6) **Arthur:** Arthwys ap Mar
7) **Ban:** Bran Hen
8) **Bedevere/Bedwyr/Owen Lawgoch:** Owen Ddantgwyn
9) **Bors:** Cincar
10) **Carados/Caradoc Vreichvras:** Cerdic/Ceredic ap Mar
11) **Cador:** Keidyaw ap Arthwys
12) **Custennin Cerneu:** Ceneu ap Coel
13) **Culhwch/Einion:** Einion ap Mar
14) **Ector:** Einion Yrth
15) **Eda Elyn Mawr:** Ida
16) **Elaine:** Gwenllian
17) **Eleuther:** Eleuther ap Arthwys
18) **Erec/Gereint:** Gereint of Damnonia
19) **Galahad ap Lancelot:** Gwallawg ap Llaenauc
20) **Gawain:** Gabran
21) **Gorlois:** Gorlais
22) **Griflet/Cynwyl ap Cynvelyn:** Cynwyd Cynwydion ap Cynbelin ap Arthwys
23) **Gwydre ap Arthur:** Gwythre ap Greidol ap Arthwys
24) **Igraine:** Gwenllian
25) **Kay/Cai Hir:** Cadwallon Law Hir
26) **Kyduan ap Arthur:** Cynvelyn ap Arthwys
27) **Lady of the Lake/Vivianne:** Coventina's Well
28) **Lamorak:** Llywarch Hen
29) **Lancelot/Eliwlod/Llwch Lleaminauc:** Llaenauc
30) **Leodegraunce:** Laoghaire
31) **Llacheu/Loholt ap Arthur:** Eleuther ap Arthwys
32) **Lot of Lothian:** Llaenauc
33) **Mabon ap Modron:** Madog ap Morydd
34) **Mark:** Cinmarc

35) **Melegaunt/Melwas:** Maelgwyn
36) **Merlin Emrys:** Pabo Post Prydain
37) **Merlin the wild:** Myrdinn ap Madog
38) **Mordred/Modred/Medraut:** Morydd ap Mar
39) **Morgan/Morgana:** St Madrun
40) **Niniane:** St Nyfaine
41) **Osla:** Octha
42) **Owen:** Owain ap Urien
43) **Perceval/Peredur ap Ebrauc:** Peredur ap Eleuther
44) **Taliesin:** Taliesin
45) **Tristan:** Drest
46) **Uriens:** Urien Rheged
47) **Uther Pendragon/Iubher:** Mar of Iubher
48) **Vortigern the Elder:** Cunedda Gwledig
49) **Vortigern Vortineu:** Ceneu
50) **Vortimer:** Mar ap Ceneu

The Dream of Rhonabwy
Arthur's descendants

The Arthurian story The Dream of Rhonabwy features the descendant of Arthwys ap Mar. The Mabinogion tale The Dream of Rhonabwy is set hundreds of years after Arthur's reign and may well be the first example of a time travel story as the eponymous character goes back to Arthur's court.

The central character, Rhonabwy, is one of Madog's retainers sent to bring in Madog's rebellious brother Iowerth Goch ap Maredudd.

His titular dream contrasts his own time with the grandeur of King Arthur's period.

The Dream of Rhonabwy (Welsh: Breuddwyd Rhonabwy) is a Middle Welsh prose tale. Set during the reign of Madog ap Maredudd, prince of Powys (died 1160), it is dated to the late 12th or 13th century. It survives in only one manuscript, the Red Book of Hergest, and has been associated with the Mabinogion since its publication by Lady Charlotte Guest in the 19th century.

The frame story tells that Madog sends Rhonabwy and two companions to find the prince's rebellious brother Iorwerth.

One night during the pursuit they seek shelter with Heilyn the Red, but find his house filthy and his beds full of fleas. Lying down on a yellow ox-skin, Rhonabwy experiences a vision of Arthur and his time. Serving as his guide is one of Arthur's followers, Iddawg the Churn of Britain, so called because he sparked the Battle of Camlann when he distorted the king's messages of peace he was supposed to deliver to the enemy Medrawd (Mordred). Iddawg introduces Rhonabwy and his friends to Arthur, who regrets that Wales has been inherited by such tiny men.

Iddawg reveals that Arthur's men are assembled to meet the Saxons at the Battle of Mount Badon. However, Arthur is more concerned with a game of gwyddbwyll (a chess-like board game) he is playing against his follower Owain mab Urien (Ywain).

218

While they play, messengers arrive declaring that Arthur's squires are attacking Owain's "ravens"; when Owain asks that this be stopped Arthur only responds, "your move."

Finally Owain orders his ravens to attack Arthur's servants; when Arthur asks him to call them off, Owain says "your move, lord." Eventually Arthur crushes the chess pieces into dust, and the two declare peace between their forces. After this the Saxons send a contingent asking for a truce, which Arthur grants after consulting his advisors. Cai (Kay) declares that any who wish to follow Arthur should come to Cornwall. The noise of the troops moving wakes Rhonabwy, who realizes he has slept for three days.

Madog was eventually succeeded by his son Owain Brogyntyn. He never succeeded to Britain, Wales or even Powys like his great ancestors. But as Lord of Edeyrnion, Castle Brogyntyn in Oswestry and Dinmael (The King's Fort) the bloodline was not completely without a kingdom. He may not have wanted the Norman kings to know about it, but from his king's fort and his castle, Owain Brogyntyn was still very much a king.

He was succeeded by his son Gruffydd, he by David and he by another Madog who took the surname Hendower meaning Old Tower. Madog Hendower married Gwenllian (the same name as King Arthur's mother) and their son was David Hendower.

David, the descendant of King Arthur, married Margaret De Cornwall, whose ancestors were the Dukes of Cornwall descended from the Plantagenet King Henry II.

Eventually the Hendower family produced no male heirs and married into the Cornish Tre-cardhen (Tregarthen) family of Madron, Penzance.

Madron was named after St Madron, King Arthur's aunt and the Morgan Le Fay of legend. The Tregarthens were the Sheriffs of Cornwall.

The family pedigree, which traces to the author, is as follows:

219

Descent from King Arthur

1. Arthwys ap Mar, Arthur King of Britain, Dux Bellorum (475AD) ~ Cywair of Ireland
2. Cinbelin Prince of Dyfed, Ebrauc and Dumnonia (C510AD)
3. Cynwyd Prince of Dyfed, Ebrauc and Dumnonia (C540AD)
4. Cadrod Calchfynedd King of Calchfynedd (C570AD)
5. Llywarch Prince of Calchfynedd (C600AD)
6. Dwynyg Prince of Calchfynedd (C620AD)
7. Gwair Prince of Calchfynedd (C640AD)
8. Tegid Prince of Calchfynedd (C670AD)
9. Algwyn Prince of Calchfynedd (C700AD)
10. Sandef Prince of Calchfynedd (C740AD)
11. Ellifer Prince of Calchfynedd (C760AD)
12. Gwriad Prince of Powys (C780AD)
13. Merfyn King of Gwynedd (C800AD)
14. Rhodri Mawr King of the Britons (820AD)
15. Cadell King of the Britons (854AD)
16. Hywell Dda of Deheubarth King of the Britons (880AD)
17. Owain of Deheubarth King of the Britons (C950)
18. Maredudd King of the Britons (C970AD)
19. Ancharad Queen of the Britons (C1020)
20. Bleddyn King of the Britons (C1050)
21. Maredudd King of the Britons (C1080)
22. Madog King of the Britons (C1130) - Ruler featured in Arthurian tale the Dream of Rhonabwy

The house of Dinmael
23. Owain Brogyntyn of Edeirnon and Dinmael (1160)
24. Gruffydd Gwledig of Edeirnon and Dinmael (C1200)
25. David Gwledig of Edeirnon and Dinmael (C1230)
26. Madog Gwledig of Edeirnon and Dinmael (C1260)
27. David Hendwr of Edeirnon and Dinmael (C1300)
28. David De Hendower of Edeirnon and Dinmael (C1330)
29. Thomas De Hendower of Edeirnon and Dinmael (C1370)
30. Richard De Hendower of Edeirnon and Dinmael (C1390)
31. Honor Hendower (1432) ~ Thomas Tregarthen

Author's descent from house of Dinmael
32. John Tregarthen (C1460)
33. John Tregarthen (C1500)
34. Nyclis Tregarthen (C1530)
35. Nyclis Tregarthen (C1560)
36. Richard Tregarthen (C1590)
37. Richard Tregarthen (C1620)
38. William Tregarthen (C1650)
39. William Tregarthen (C1680)
40. Hugh Tregarthen (1705)
41. Joyce Tregarthen (C1725) ~ Tobias Legg
42. James Legg (c1740)
43. Tobias Legg (C1770)
44. Zacharias Legg (C1800)
45. Jane Legg (1820) ~ Frederick Woodcock
46. Phoebe Woodcock (1861) ~ Frederick Woodcock
47. Violet Stephens (1897) ~ William Henry Nelson
48. Charles James Nelson (1923)
49. Carol Ann Nelson (1951) ~ David Keegan
50. Simon Keegan, the author (1979)
- Poppy Keegan (2009)
- Edward Keegan (2013)

Prince William, Prince Charles and the Queen are descended from Arthur of Dyfed via his daughter Nest down through Rhodri Mawr's line. They are also descended from Arthwys ap Mar via Cadrod's son Esbwys. The two lines converge with King Henry VII's grandfather Maredudd.

Epilogue

Book One, Pennine Dragon argues very simply that the warrior leader King Arthur, as described by Nennius, Aneirin, Llywarch Hen and Taliesin should be identified with the King of Ebrauc Arthwys ap Mar. On this basic historical level he was the Dux Bellorum who defended the area surrounding Hadrian's Wall and York.

We also explored the family trees and mythological themes in works such as Culhwch, the Saints' Lives, Geoffrey of Monmouth and Chretien and met characters from the Arthurian legends.

Book Two Bearman Pendragon is an entirely different hypothesis, that this Arthwys ap Mar was not only a king of the North, but he also conquered Dyfed, Cornwall, and ventured to Scotland, Ireland and France.

Book One establishes Arthwys as the historic King Arthur, Book Two proposes he was every bit the national emperor.
The reader can take Book One in isolation or they can take on board the two works.

I write this on the 1,500th anniversary of Arthwys ap Mar's victory at Badon in 516AD and hope he finally earns his true place in the history books.

Simon Keegan

About The Author

Simon Keegan was born in Liverpool in 1979 of Irish, Scottish, Cornish, Breton, Welsh and Swedish ancestry.

He has been a professional journalist for 20 years and currently works for the Daily Mirror. He has also worked as a sub editor for the Metro, Daily Star and Daily Express.

Simon was editor of the Salford Advertiser and Prestwich Advertiser and has also worked for magazines such as The Big Issue in the North and local newspapers such as the Stockport Express and Rochdale Observer.

He has also appeared on various TV and radio shows as well as judging the UK's largest live music contest.

Simon is married with two children and in his spare time teaches a Karate and Jujutsu class in Manchester city centre.

In pursuit of the Arthurian legends, he has travelled from Scotland to Cornwall, Ireland to Brittany, Wales to York and all points between.

PENNINE DRAGON

PENNINE DRAGON

PENNINE DRAGON

Lightning Source UK Ltd.
Milton Keynes UK
UKOW06f0212150416

272291UK00002B/125/P